THE EVERYTHING BUBBLE:

The Endgame For Central Bank Policy

GRAHAM SUMMERS, MBA

ISBN: 978-1974634064

Visit: www.theeverythingbubble.com

For my wife, Lucia.

CONTENTS

INTRODUCTION

This book is divided into two sections titled: *How We Got Here* and *What's to Come*.

How We Got Here concerns the creation and evolution of the United States (US) financial system, starting with the creation of the current US central bank, the Federal Reserve, in 1913, and running some 100+ years up to the creation of the current bubble in sovereign bonds, which I call "**The Everything Bubble**" (more on this shortly).

I want to stress that this section of the book takes a "big picture" approach to its analysis. So, if you're looking for dense, intensive economic theory or an exploration into the nuances of things like labor cost per unit or straight-line depreciation methodology, this is NOT the book for you.

Rather, we will be focusing on the key individuals, policy decisions, and economic themes involved in the development of our current financial system. Who were the people involved? Why did they do what they did? And, how did their decisions shape the US financial system and economy over the last 100+ years?

Having said that, some portions of this book will be technical in nature. Whenever this is the case, I'll provide a disclaimer preceding the technical section so you can simply skip ahead if you're not interested.

By the time you finish reading this section of the book, you'll know more about money, the US financial system, banking, and the financial markets than 99% of the general public. At the very least, you'll have a solid framework for analyzing why things are the way they are.

The second half of this book titled, *What's to Come*, is meant to provide a blueprint for what will be unfolding in the future, both in terms of financial "events" and the Federal Reserve's policy response to them.

If you have followed my work prior to this book, you may know my primary concern today is that the US financial system is heading towards a financial crisis that will make the 2008 meltdown look like a picnic.

This is not some "doom and gloom" forecast about how the world is ending… rather, this is an almost obvious conclusion based on the fact that the Federal Reserve has dealt with the bursting of every asset bubble of the last 20 years by creating another, larger bubble in a more senior asset class.

From 1996 to 1999, the US financial system experienced a bubble in Technology stocks called the Tech Bubble.

This bubble burst in 2000. The Federal Reserve chose to deal with it by creating another, larger bubble in US real estate: a more senior asset class with broader implications for the US financial system.

From 2003 to 2008, this bubble grew until it burst, resulting in the Great Financial Crisis of 2008. And, the Federal Reserve dealt with this by creating… you guessed it… another, even larger bubble in US sovereign bonds or Treasuries.

And, because these bonds are the bedrock of the US financial system, or the "risk free rate" against which every asset class is measured, when the Fed did this it created a bubble in literally *EVERYTHING*.

As a result, today we are in, what I call, **The Everything Bubble.**

When this bubble bursts, the Fed will be forced to engage in even more extreme policy responses. The reason is simply that the entire political/financial structure of the United States today has been built on the back of ever-cheaper debt (bonds are debt) for the last 40 years. So, when the US bond market begins to blow up, the political class will be calling on the Federal Reserve to engage in **<u>extreme</u>** interventions to maintain the status quo.

I outline all of these policies, as well as their implications for the US financial system in the second half of this book, ***What's To Come***.

Significant portions of ***What's To Come*** will be referring to issues and concepts we first discuss in ***How We Got Here***. So, while it might be tempting to start with the second half of the book and skip the historical stuff, doing so will leave you at something of a disadvantage.

Finally, do know that any time I make a bold claim, I'll be backing it up with historical precedent or with a very carefully presented argument based on verifiable facts. In fact, this book is the culmination of over 10 years of intensive research-based analysis and engagement with all of the above topics. In other words, it is literally a distillation of a decade of work.

This knowledge is now yours.

PART 1:
How We Got Here

CHAPTER 1:
How Debt Became Money

"FOUR DOLLARS!?! GOOD GOD ALMIGHTY! I DON'T LIKE 'EM THAT MUCH!"

I'm in a grocery store, in the snack aisle, watching an elderly woman lose her mind over the price of a package of cookies.

With no offence meant and from a contextual standpoint, I'm guessing she's in her '70s, which means she was born sometime in the 1940s.

During the course of her life, she's lived through the end of World War II, the American civil rights movement, the moon landing, the John F. Kennedy assassination, the 1973 Oil Crisis, the end of the Cold War/ fall of the Berlin Wall, the creation of the Internet and more... much more.

She's also seen the price of everything rise virtually non-stop. Which might very well explain why she's currently screaming at a package of cookies.

The cookies themselves are nothing but butter, sugar, eggs, flour and maybe a little salt.

Over the last 70 years, advances in farming and technology have made it easier to harvest and produce all of these items.

And yet, during this woman's lifetime, **the cost of these basic ingredients has risen by an average of more than 500%.**

When she was a young girl in the 1950s, sugar cost less than 10 cents a pound, a dozen eggs cost 60 cents, butter cost 72 cents a pound, and flour cost less than 5 cents a pound. Please do not forget we are talking <u>cents</u> per <u>pound.</u>

Today, the price of a pound of flour is up 940% to 52 cents a pound. Sugar is up 560%. Butter is up 409%. And the price of a dozen eggs is up 248%. And, we are not even talking "organic."

Throw in chemical preservatives that increase the cookies' shelf life, the cost of packaging, and the corporate mandate to maximize profits, and all of a sudden you've got a $4+ package of cookies and a very upset senior citizen who won't be snacking on cookies this afternoon.

Of course, I am not trying to tease the old woman. I'm old enough to be playing the *"when I was younger [insert random good or service] cost only [insert much lower price]"* game too.

Heck, *everyone* can. The prices for virtually *everything* have risen almost non-stop for the last 100 years. Whether you were born in the 1930s, '40s, '50s, '60s, '70s, '80s, etc. the price you pay for the things you need to live (food, energy, housing) have generally risen throughout your lifetime.

Or have they?

Anyone who sits down and thinks about the near continuous increase in prices of everyday items realizes that it makes no sense. Cookies don't taste any better today than they did 10 years ago… or 70 years ago for that matter.

The same goes for our clothes, housing, and many other items (computers and technology are two of the few exceptions). Indeed, most people I know argue that nothing is built to last anymore. And yet these same items cost *more* today than they did in the past.

Why is everything so much more expensive?

It's not. The price of things hasn't actually risen. What's happened is that the US dollar, the currency we use to *pay* for these items, has fallen in purchasing power.

But, what is purchasing power?

Purchasing power is the proverbial "bang for your buck," or how much of something you can buy for a single unit of currency.

In the United States, one dollar today is worth roughly 10% of what it was worth when the upset cookie lady was a young girl. And, it's worth only 4% of what it was worth in 1913.

Below is one of the ugliest charts you'll ever see (Chart 1). They don't show this chart in school for good reason.

Chart 1. Purchasing Power of the US Dollar (1913-2016).

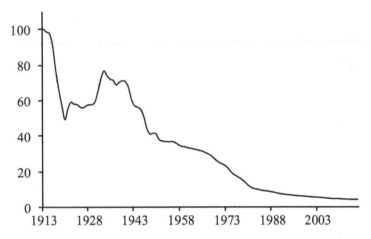

Note: Data adapted from Federal Reserve Bank of St. Louis (2017)[1]

You'll note that this chart starts in 1913. What happened in 1913?

The United States' Central Bank, called the Federal Reserve, or "the Fed," (herein referred to interchangeably) was created.

Unless you work in finance, usually whenever you start talking about "the Fed" and how it has destroyed the value of the US dollar, most people start looking at you like you're talking about UFOs or Bigfoot.

However, the above chart is not some crazy conspiracy theory. It is real. In fact, I got the data **FROM ONE OF THE FED'S OWN WEBSITES.**

Of course, we cannot lay everything at the Fed's feet. Two other major US policies are responsible for the US dollar being worth only 4% of what it used to be.

Those two items are:

1) Former President Franklin Delano Roosevelt taking the US dollar off the Gold Standard in 1933.

2) Former President Richard Nixon completely severing the US dollar from any link to gold in 1971.

I've added these items to Chart 2.

Chart 2. Purchasing Power of the US Dollar with Historical Notes (1913-2016).

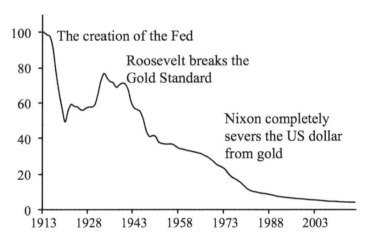

Note: Data adapted from Federal Reserve Bank of St. Louis (2017)[1]

Of course, the economic history of the United States in the 20th century involved a lot more than this. However, these three items are the **most important developments** regarding how our current financial system works.

With that in mind, we're going to explore all three. For those of you who are keen to move on to more recent developments like the Housing Bubble, bear with me for a few more pages, as this background information is going to be referenced repeatedly throughout the book.

By the time you finish this chapter you'll have a better understanding of the US financial system than 99% of people.

What is the Fed?

You've probably heard about the Fed on TV or in the news. Most people associate the phrase "the Fed" with the economy and the US dollar.

Those of us who are more involved in the financial industry know the Fed is responsible for managing the US economy by controlling the flow of money into and out the US financial system via interest rates.

What few people know, however, is that the Fed is NOT actually part of the US government.

Wait, what? You mean to tell me that the US' Central Bank... the bank in charge of printing US dollars... *isn't* officially a part of the US government?

Yep. If you go to the Federal Reserve's website you'll note that it has a .gov web address. (https://www.federalreserve.gov/).

However, this is not actually "the Fed's" website. This is the website for "The Board of Governors of the Federal Reserve System," or the *management team* that leads the Federal Reserve.

Nowhere does the site state *precisely* what the Fed is or how it *really* operates (though there are some articles providing a rough outline of its activities). Instead, there are pictures and biographies of the Fed Board of Governors as well as articles detailing Fed policy and research.

"So what?" you may ask, *"Why is this weird?"*

Imagine if Coca-Cola's website didn't mention that the company is a publicly traded stock nor what the company does in any great detail. Imagine if instead Coca-Cola's website focused on the company's board of directors and the policies they employ at the company.

This would be the equivalent of the Federal Reserve's .gov website.

Now, the Federal Reserve DOES maintain another website that focuses more on the Federal Reserve Banking System's services. However, this website is NOT a .gov site, but a .org site: https://www.frbservices.org/.

This means that the Fed's actual operations are NOT controlled or dictated by the US Federal Government.

Indeed, under the "About Us" section of the Fed's .org website the Fed explains what it is:

> "A Bank for the Government
>
> Additionally, the Federal Reserve acts as a fiscal agent or bank to the federal government by providing financial services to the United States Department of Treasury and by selling and redeeming government securities such as Savings Bonds and Treasury bills."
>
> Source: Federal Reserve Bank Services[2]

12

Note that the Fed says it *"acts…as a bank __to__ the federal government"*, not *"__of__"* the federal government. And, no, this is not meant to be a grammatical mistake.

This means the federal government *uses* the Fed, but it doesn't *own or run* the Fed. For all intents and purposes, the Fed is no more controlled by the United States government than any other organization the government uses for a specific service.

Hold on… what you are saying is that the United States' Central Bank, which is in charge of printing money and steering the economy *isn't* a part of the government?

Yep.

But surely, the government must decide who runs the Fed?

Nope.

Well, from a technical standpoint, the President of the United States *does* choose the Chair of the Federal Reserve's Board of Governors.

However, even this setup is something of a farce as the candidates for Fed Chair are limited to the Fed's Board of Governors… all of whom are picked by the Federal Reserve banks themselves (more on this shortly).

Put another way, the President picks the Fed Chair from a group of candidates already picked out by the Fed. This is hardly what you'd call government oversight.

I'm not making this stuff up. Few people on the planet know who really runs the Fed as an organization. And all of them have major Non-Disclosure Agreements in place.

I will say that for those of us outside those circles, only two things are publicly known about the Fed and its operations:

1) Since the Fed was created, the US dollar has lost 96% of its purchasing power.

2) The people who created the Fed in 1913 were representatives of the wealthiest, most powerful banking dynasties in the world.

The Most Expensive "Duck Hunt" in History

By now, some of you are probably thinking that this book is either a work of fiction or a composite of conspiracy theories without anything to back it up. Well, buckle up, because I'm about to give you serious content for dinner conversation or your next tweet.

The blueprint for the United States Central Bank or Federal Reserve was laid out by six or seven men (depending on whose account you trust) during a private retreat at Jekyll Island off the coast of Georgia in 1910.

Again, this is not some conspiracy; the Federal Reserve itself is quite open about who these men were, and the purpose of their meeting.

The men were:

1) Nelson Aldrich, Senator of Rhode Island and Republican "whip," also Chairman of the National Monetary Commission, business associate of J.P. Morgan and father-in-law to John D. Rockefeller, Jr.

2) Abraham Andrew, Assistant Secretary of the Treasury.

3) Frank Vanderlip, President of National City Bank of New York, the most powerful bank in the United States at the time, representing William Rockefeller and the international investment house of Kuhn, Loeb, & Co.

4) Henry Davidson, Senior Partner at the J.P. Morgan Company.

5) Charles Norton, President of J.P. Morgan's First National Bank of New York.

6) Benjamin Strong, head of J.P. Morgan's Bankers Trust Company.

7) Paul Warburg, partner of Kuhn, Loeb, & Co., representative of the Rothschild banking dynasty in England and France, and brother to Max Warburg who was head of the Warburg banking consortium in Germany and the Netherlands.

Together, these seven men represented interests that controlled **one fourth of the world's entire wealth.**

That is not a typo. These individuals represented the four most powerful groups in the Anglo-American banking world. They were:

From the United States	From Europe
The Rockefellers	The Rothschilds
The Morgans	The Warburgs

The meeting was scheduled and publicized as a group of political/ financial elites who were friendly with one another going on a "duck hunt."

The reality was that Senator Aldrich organized this "duck hunt" specifically with the intention of developing a new banking system for the United States. Like all plans for major reform the intentions here were both noble and corrupt.

On the more noble side, the United States had just emerged from its first *national* banking crisis in 1907. Without going into too much detail here, this crisis can be summed up as follows:

1) A new type of financial firm called a "Trust" had grown increasingly popular as an alternative to traditional banks.

2) Trusts received their charters for doing business from individual states, NOT from the Federal Government (remember this is pre-1933 so there was no centralized regulation for banks or Federal Deposit Insurance Corporation).

3) Trusts were not part of the formal New York banking system and so were loosely regulated.

4) Because Trusts were loosely regulated, they tended to generate larger, riskier loans than traditional banks. They also tended to maintain less capital as a buffer for dealing with crises.

5) Trusts began generating massive loans to stock traders and other financial speculators from 1905-1907.

6) In 1907, several major stock traders blew up, taking down a number of smaller Trusts (again, Trusts made riskier loans and maintained less capital as a buffer).

7) A contagion ensued and the entire financial system began to implode.

The only thing that brought the United States banking system back from the brink was an all-night meeting that took place in J.P. Morgan's private library (Morgan was head of the largest banking dynasty in the United States at the time).

In simple terms, Morgan locked the heads of the major New York banks in his library and effectively threatened, bribed, and cajoled them into offering liquidity to prop up the banking system. By the following morning, Morgan had written agreements from the bank heads and money started flowing back into the market.

In this context, the 1910 meeting at Jekyll Island was meant to stop another 1907-type Crisis from ever happening again. The participants blamed the crisis on loose regulation and the lack of a central banking system that could provide liquidity during periods of market turmoil.

The less noble aspect of the meeting was the fact that all of those involved were Anglo-American financial elites who would greatly profit from the creation of this new centralized banking system.

Indeed, by centralizing the system, the individuals involved were cutting out their competitors AND granting themselves greater control over the United States banking system.

Over the next nine days, they hashed out a plan that would eventually morph into the current Federal Reserve System of banking.

The initial plan had five key attributes:

1) The bank would be called "the Federal Reserve" thereby avoiding the terms "Central" and "Bank" (at this point the United States had already had two Central Banks and neither had been popular nor lasted very long).

2) The Federal Reserve system would be a centralized banking system comprised of 12 regional banks located in Boston, New York, Philadelphia, Cleveland, Richmond, Atlanta, Chicago, St. Louis, Minneapolis, Kansas

City, Dallas, and San Francisco.

3) Each regional bank would have its own President, but ultimate decision making would be made by the Fed's Board of Governors: semi-elected officials who would meet in Washington D.C. to coordinate monetary policy and set interest rates (more on this later).

4) All 12 regional banks would pool their reserves and set nation-wide standards for leverage, capital and loans; thereby minimizing the risks of bank runs and failure.

And, finally…

5) The Federal Reserve would take over the issuance of ALL money in the United States, marking the first time in the country's history that money would be produced solely by privately held banks, NOT the United States government.

It took three years and various political schemes to get a form of this plan put into law. But on December 23, 1913, the Federal Reserve Act was passed in Congress.

From then on, the Federal Reserve was the United States' Central Bank and the US dollar was a "Federal Reserve Note."

See for yourself:

Missed it? Look at the top of the bill:

FEDERAL RESERVE NOTE

So that explains how the Fed was created: the first point on Chart 2.

However, you'll note that it wasn't until Franklin Delano Roosevelt broke the Gold Standard in 1933 that the US dollar really began to drop in purchasing power.[*]

Which is Riskier, Farming or Day-Trading?

We are taught in school that Franklin Delano Roosevelt was a hero who saved the financial system and ended the Great Depression. However, I can tell you that the people teaching this have little understanding of business or the economy.

The view that Roosevelt somehow waved a magic wand and saved the system is a fairy tale similar to that of the Easter Bunny leaving us candy on Easter morning. The reality is that as far as the US economy was concerned, Roosevelt acted more like a third world dictator than the leader of the free world.

To fully understand what I mean by this, you first need to have some context.

---

[*] There is one exception to this trend, that occurred between 1918 and 1933 when the US dollar strengthened in purchasing power. However, this had little to do with the Fed.

In the aftermath of World War I, many countries in Europe abandoned any link between their currencies and gold. As soon as they did this, they began printing vast amounts of their currencies.

The currency debasement resulted in the British Pound, French Franc, and German Reichsmark losing considerable value against the US dollar. This, combined with capital fleeing Europe for the United States, pushed the US dollar higher for a time.

In the 1920s, the United States was still largely an agricultural economy with 21% of the American workforce employed on farms.

Of course, farming is an extremely risky business. Farmers take on huge debts and are often just one bad crop away from bankruptcy (machinery, land and other necessary items are usually financed by debt).

To make matters worse, the United States' agricultural economy was financed by an extremely fragmented banking system in which two thirds of all banks in the country were small, rural banks servicing towns with populations of 2,500 people or less.

Most of these banks were not members of the new Federal Reserve banking system and so could not easily request emergency lending if a crisis hit. And, since most of these smaller banks were often the only bank in town, if a farmer defaulted on a particularly large loan the bank was in serious trouble.

Against this backdrop, you also need to know that at this time the US dollar was directly linked to the price of gold at $20.67 per ounce. Part of this link **required that each and every US dollar was fully convertible to gold.**

So if you had US dollars in your wallet, you could walk into a bank and exchange them for actual physical gold.

Similarly, if you had money deposited in a bank, you could choose to withdraw it in the form of US dollars *or* gold.

Obviously there is a limited amount of gold in the world. And, United States banks owned only a portion of it. So if a serious bank run began, and Americans started demanding their deposits back in gold, it wouldn't take long to deplete the banks' reserves and start a crisis.

This was *especially* true for smaller banks that owned little, if any gold.

Put simply, the United States banking system in the 1920s was a highly fragmented, loosely regulated mess that was one major recession away from failure.

Unfortunately, that recession was about to be triggered by a massive stock market crash.

Indeed, if the United States banking system was a powder keg waiting to go off in the 1920s, it was the 1929 Crash that lit the fuse.

You see, rural banks weren't the only banks engaged in risky lending practices in the 1920s. Numerous New York-based firms, particularly those operating outside of the Federal Reserve banking system, were lending out absolutely insane amounts of money to… **stock traders**.

I emphasize this on purpose. Lending money to traders is even riskier than lending money to farmers. Farmers at least have land, machinery and the like to act as collateral on their loans. Traders have their trading accounts… which can go to zero in a single day with a few wrong trades.

This was particularly true in the 1920s when the process of using borrowed money to buy stocks (also called "buying on margin") was **completely unregulated.**

At this time, it wasn't unusual for brokers to lend their clients 50%, 70%, sometimes even 90% of the money for an investment.

So let's say you had $10,000 in your account but you wanted to buy $100,000 worth of ABC Company's stock; your broker would be willing to lend you that $90,000 without even asking for collateral on the loan. Pretty neat, huh?

Now, investing with borrowed money is great when your trades go well. But, if you're trading using a ton of borrowed money and a trade goes against you, it takes very little for you to completely wipe out your capital... and potentially take down the bank that loaned you the money.

To return to our example, with $90,000 borrowed on a $100,000 trade, the stock only needs to fall 10% for you to have wiped out your entire account (10% x $100,000 =$10,000).

Enter the stock market crash.

Americans Go For Gold...

In late October 1929, the United States stock market lost 23% of its value over the course of two days. It was, up until that point, the single worst stock market crash in the country's history.

The crash wiped out countless traders as well as the New York banks that had loaned them money. Before the year 1929 was over, 650 banks had failed.

As news of the crash hit national headlines, Americans began going to their banks and demanding their deposits back. This might seem a bit excessive to us today, but you have to remember that at this point in US history, there **was no deposit insurance** (the Federal Deposit Insurance Corporation, or FDIC, was created in 1933).

Put another way, before 1933, if the bank where you kept your savings went under, **you lost everything**.

As a result of this, Americans were naturally wary of keeping their money in banks. And, since the US dollar had already lost a fifth of its purchasing power since the Fed's creation in 1913, Americans weren't overly keen on keeping their money in US dollars either.

So, they started pulling their money from banks in the form of gold.

This presented banks with a massive problem. As I mentioned before, there was a limited amount of gold in the banking system. Thus, even if a bank had joined the Federal Reserve banking system and had access to emergency capital, **this still didn't mean the bank could easily acquire more gold.**

The United States rapidly entered a full-scale banking crisis. Strikingly, at the depth of the Depression, it's estimated that banks were failing at a pace of more than 75 per week, or more than 10 per day!

The Fed, desperate to stop this, actually *RAISED* interest rates in 1930. The goal here was:

1) To make the US dollar more attractive as a storehouse of value (gold doesn't pay any interest).

2) To stop Americans from pulling money from their banks (in order to collect the interest on US dollars, the money would need to be in a bank account).

The Fed failed. In fact, raising rates only deepened the recession as raising interest rates made debt more expensive (this "mistake" would later be used to justify the Fed's extreme actions in response to the 2008 housing crisis as we'll cover later in this book).

Americans kept demanding their money in gold. Banks kept running out of gold. Borrowers who owed the banks money kept defaulting on their loans. And, the banks kept going under.

In 1931 over 2,000 banks failed. That's a rate of roughly <u>five</u> banks failing per day.

Looking at this situation, it was clear something had to change. According to then-President Franklin Delano Roosevelt, that "something" was the US financial system's reliance on gold.

The Largest Wealth Confiscation in United States History

In 1933, Franklin Delano Roosevelt began the process of removing the link between the US dollar and gold.

First he closed the banks for four days. During this time, NO ONE could get his or her money out.

Then, he forbade the banks from exporting gold abroad (international banks that stored money in the United States were also asking for their money back in the form of gold). Roosevelt wanted to keep as much gold as possible under the United States' control.

Finally, Roosevelt demanded that all United States citizens *turn in* their gold to the federal government.

Yes, the President of the United States *demanded* that Americans hand over their personal property to the United States government. Don't believe me? Look up Executive Order 6102, which Roosevelt later issued making gold ownership illegal.

Surprisingly-or not- academic historians like to defend this action by saying *"he was trying to stop a massive crisis, so the move was justified."*

I'm not so sure about that one. Let's imagine the financial reality Americans faced during this period.

Over 1,000 banks were failing *per year* going into 1933.... and the President was *demanding* that Americans give the United States government their gold... thereby **forcing them to own US**

dollars... dollars that would almost certainly have to be kept in the banks... that were, again, failing at a pace of 3+ per week.

Does this seem like a justified move to you?

Of course, as much as Franklin Delano Roosevelt is glorified, few actually point out that virtually NO ONE went along with his scheme. Americans weren't stupid. And they weren't about to hand over gold, which had been a storehouse of value for 5,000 years, to own US dollars that had already lost 20% of their value in the preceding decades.

So, Franklin Delano Roosevelt passed Executive Order 6102, making it *illegal* for Americans to privately own gold.

Yes, this was an *Executive Order...* Congress wasn't involved in it.

I realize that the implications of this might be lost on some, so let me put it this way: Franklin Delano Roosevelt made it a CRIME to keep your money in gold... a crime punishable by up to 10 years in prison and a fine of up to $10,000 ($185,000 in today's money).

Are you still sure this move is *justified*?

This, in effect, FORCED Americans to store their hard earned money **in US dollars** (other asset class alternatives were disastrous: stocks and real estate were both collapsing).

Not yet finished, the US government then passed *The Gold Reserve Act* which permitted the government to pay its debts in *US dollars,* not gold: a move that allowed the government to pay its debt while keeping its gold.

Still not finished, Roosevelt then raised the official price of gold from $20.67 to $35.00 per ounce.

This last point is the most critical one.

The "Savior" of the Financial System Erases 70% of ALL Savings

When Roosevelt *raised* the price of gold, he was effectively *devaluing* the US dollar. An ounce of gold is an ounce of gold. So raising the price of an ounce of gold means *lowering* the value of the currency in which you are pricing gold.

Roosevelt did this. And not by a little… by over **69%.**

Now, academic economists will try to give various clever explanations for this. Explanations aside, at the end of the day:

1) The Franklin Delano Roosevelt-lead government confiscated Americans' gold.

2) The Franklin Delano Roosevelt-lead government FORCED Americans to store their wealth in US dollars or US dollar-denominated assets.

3) The Franklin Delano Roosevelt-lead government devalued the US dollar by over 69%.

This is why I wrote that Roosevelt acted more like a dictator in a third world country than the leader of the free world. Culturally the shock of these policies took years to overcome.

Chart 3 chronicles the decline in the purchasing power of the US dollar following Franklin Delano Roosevelt ending the Gold Standard. As you can see, the US dollar nosedived and hasn't looked back ever since. All told, it lost 50% of its purchasing power by the time the children of the Great Depression became adults.

Chart 3. Purchasing Power of the US Dollar (1933-2016).

Note: Data adapted from Federal Reserve Bank of St. Louis (2017)[1]

From 1933 until 1964, it was illegal for Americans to own gold unless you had a special license. During that period, everyone (the upset cookie lady included), was stuck owning US dollars that were continually losing their purchasing power.

As much as we can blame Franklin Delano Roosevelt for that chart, it's important to note that the US dollar was still *technically* pegged to gold at $35 per ounce (though the only entities that could convert their dollars into gold were foreign Central Banks).

So, technically, gold remained the ultimate backstop of the financial system. And since the US dollar remained convertible to gold by Central Banks, there was a limit to how much money printing the Federal Reserve could employ without consequence (if the Fed printed too many US dollars resulting in the US dollar losing its purchasing power too rapidly, eventually foreign Central Banks would begin converting their US dollars into gold).

Then along came Richard Nixon.

Nixon's Biggest Scandal Had Nothing To Do With Watergate

Richard Nixon is the only President to have resigned from office. That alone has resulted in him being the single most vilified President in American History.

However, the damage caused by the Watergate scandal (Nixon's underlings broke into the Democrat National Committee's office at the Watergate hotel) pales in comparison to the damage Nixon caused by completely severing the link between the US dollar and gold in 1971.

Put it this way…one of these scandals led to the *political* bankruptcy of the Nixon administration and Nixon's resignation; the other opened the door to endless money printing/ debt issuance and the *financial* bankruptcy **of the entire country.**

You see, before Nixon completlely severed the dollar's link to gold, Central Banks could still exchange the dollars they owned for gold. This convertibility acted as a limit on the amount of US dollars the Federal Reserve could print (since the amount of gold in the system was finite).

A secondary effect of this was that the gold link also placed a limit on the amount of debt the United States could issue since all US debt would need to be paid back in US dollars… US dollars that could then be exchanged for gold by Central Banks.

Before 1971, here's how the US debt markets worked.

1) The United States issued debt.

2) Foreign governments bought this debt via their Central Banks.

3) The United States paid the interest on this debt (as well as paying off the debt itself) in US dollars.

4) Foreign governments accrued US dollars... US dollars
    that they could exchange for gold, if they wished.

In this regard, the global currency peg to the US dollar, as well
as the US dollar's link to gold, acted as a ceiling over how much
money the United States could print as well as how much debt it
could issue.

Nixon took away this limit.

Worst of all, he did this *entirely* for political reasons: the Nixon
tapes reveal that he was personally aware that breaking the US
dollar's link to gold would have disastrous long-term effects for
the United States economy.

However, in 1971 Nixon wasn't thinking "long-term"; he was
thinking about one thing: winning the 1972 Presidential election.
And, his reelection bid was facing two major problems:

1) The unemployment rate was rising, having risen to 5.9%
    from 3.5% when Nixon took office (rising unemploy-
    ment tends to be a deal breaker in Presidential elections).

2) Despite the rise in unemployment, the Federal Reserve
    was convinced the US economy had exited the recession
    of the late '60s. So the Fed was raising rates (a policy
    that usually slows the economy).

To remedy this, the Nixon administration began putting pressure
on then-Fed Chair Arthur Burns to ease monetary policy (lower
rates and print money) in order to juice the economy and bring
down the unemployment rate.

Burns was slow to respond so at one point Nixon even threatened
(indirectly through surrogates) to have the Treasury acquire/ab-
sorb the Fed (thereby firing Burns and his associates and bringing the Federal Reserve under control of the US government).

That finally got the message through.

Burns began cutting rates in mid-1971. However, Nixon wasn't satisfied that this would produce the desired results in time for the 1972 election (it usually takes six months or more for Fed policy to have a significant impact on the economy).

And so, on August 15, 1971, Nixon held a televised address in which he announced **that the United States was ending the gold peg completely.**

I want to emphasize the abject insanity of this.

Nixon was well aware of the negative consequences of this decision. Economist Milton Friedman had explicitly told Nixon to his face behind closed doors that aggressive monetary policy would unleash inflation.

Despite this knowledge, Nixon chose to abandon the gold peg *expressly* to aid in his re-election bid. He knowingly chose to unleash inflation in order to secure a second term in the White House.

This elevates Nixon to a special level of monetary supervillain.

As much as I've vilified Franklin Delano Roosevelt's move to begin ending the Gold Standard in 1933, Nixon's move to completely end the US dollar's link to gold in 1971 was far worse.

Franklin Delano Roosevelt was at least facing a severe banking crisis and the Great Depression. Nixon was simply trying to get another term in office.

Today, Nixon, unlike Roosevelt, is remembered for being a monster. Unfortunately, it's for the wrong scandal: Watergate.

After all, which is worse… listening in on your opponents' campaign strategies, or opening the door to endless money printing/debt issuance and the eventual bankruptcy of the republic?

I'm not being hyperbolic here. The US dollar lost roughly 80% of its purchasing power after Nixon severed the gold link.

Moreover, because all US debt would now be paid exclusively in US dollars (US dollars that the Fed could print at anytime) there was technically no limit to the amount of debt the United States could issue.

See for yourself... from 1946 until 1971 when Nixon ended the gold peg, the total amount of debt in the US financial system remained close to its annual economic output or Gross Domestic Product. Moreover, throughout this period, both the United States' Gross Domestic Product and debt levels grew at roughly the same pace.

Chart 4. US Gross Domestic Product vs. US Total Debt Securities, Trillions US Dollars (1945-2016).

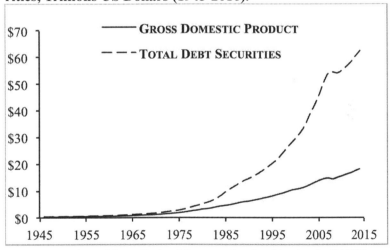

Note: Data adapted from Federal Reserve Bank of St. Louis (2017)[3]

Within a year of Nixon ending the gold peg, the slope of debt growth accelerated. Within five years, debt was growing faster than Gross Domestic Product. Within 15 years, it was growing at roughly twice the pace of Gross Domestic Product.

And in 1986, the total amount of debt in the US financial system hit 200% of the country's annual economic output.

It hasn't looked back since.

However, we're getting ahead of ourselves here… on August 16th, 1971, the day after Nixon ended the gold peg, everyone was asking one question:

"If gold is no longer the ultimate backstop for the US financial system, what is?"

Debt. Specifically, debt issued by the United States government.

Debt Becomes "Risk Free"

Without gold backing it, the US dollar was now backed by the full faith and credit of the United States government. **In simple terms, the US dollar was supported by the belief that the United States would never default on its debts.**

It had taken 58 years, but the United States financial system had shifted from gold to the US dollar and now to debt as the ultimate storehouse of value for its financial system.

Put another way, the backstop for the United States financial system had shifted from a hard asset that had stored wealth for 5,000 years (gold), to paper money (which had *always* failed), and finally to a loan made to the *same* Government that had *forced* Americans to give up their gold in the first place.

<u>Good God Almighty.</u>

Since that time, US government debt, or Treasuries have been the ultimate "risk-free" benchmark for the financial system.

That's correct. According to modern financial theory (theory based on the financial system after the Fed's creation in 1913), lending money to the United States government (buying a US Government Bond, or Treasury) **is considered the "risk free" rate of return for the financial system.**

I realize this sounds completely bonkers. After all, since when is lending money to anyone or anything considered risk free? Surely sitting on cash is less risky than lending money to the United States government?

Not after 1971.

Remember, once Nixon abandoned the gold peg completely in 1971, the US dollar was no longer backed by gold or any other finite asset.

Because of this, the Fed could print money any time it wants, *devaluing* the US dollar. So, technically speaking, your cash is at risk of losing value via Central Bank money printing/ inflation.

In this regard, the complete abandonment of any link to gold changed the risk profile of the financial system.

In a non-fiat based financial system (a system in which the currency is backed by gold or some other finite asset), the primary risk for any asset is the loss of capital (meaning you lose money because the value of the asset falls).

In contrast, in a purely fiat-based financial system (a system in which the currency is "paper money" backed by nothing) there are TWO primary risks:

1) The risk of loss of capital (meaning you lose money

because the value of the asset falls).

And...

2) The risk of loss of purchasing power via inflation
   (meaning that an investment fails to provide a return
   that exceeds the rate of inflation and so loses purchasing
   power).

In a paper money-based financial system such as the one the
United States has had since severing the US dollar's link to gold
in 1971, physical cash avoids Risk #1, but not Risk #2. In this
context, **cash is no longer a "risk-free" asset class.**

United States Government Debt, on the other hand, is supposed
to pay you a yield *based* on inflation as well as economic activity
(growth). Chart 5 shows the performance of the rate of change
in the 10-Year Treasury yield vs. the rate of change in inflation,
called the Consumer Price Index, or CPI.

**Chart 5. Year Over Year Change in US Inflation vs. 10-Year
US Treasury Yield (1971 to 2000).**

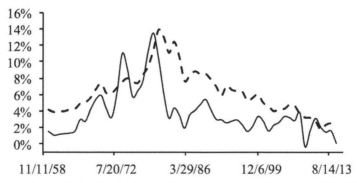

Note: Data adapted from Federal Reserve Bank of St. Louis (2017)[4]

As you can see, US Treasury yields track inflation relatively well, thereby protecting against currency devaluation or Central Bank money printing.

Of course, the correlation isn't perfect as Treasuries also move based on economic activity, trader perceptions and more. But my primary point is that Treasuries adjust for any spike in inflation. In this way, they maintain the purchasing power of your capital.

This is why modern financial theory believes buying Treasuries (lending money to the United States government) is "risk free" in terms of their relationship to inflation.

But, what about the other risk for capital in a fiat-based financial system: the risk of loss of capital (meaning the risk of losing your money altogether)? Do Treasuries manage that risk too?

The answer here is, again, related to money printing.

Because the United States government has the ability to print dollars (via the Fed), lending it money is considered to be "risk free" because no matter what happens, the government can always have the Fed print more money to pay its lenders back.

Understand, I'm not claiming I like this setup. I am merely explaining how the current financial system works. In our current system, lending money to the United States government by buying US Treasuries is considered "risk free" because these bonds pays interest based on inflation and because no matter what, the United States government can have the Fed print money to pay you back.

It took 50+ years and countless political machinations, but the Fed and the government managed to change the financial system so that what's "risk free" went from being something you own and keep in your possession (gold) to lending your money to the United States government.

During the course of this transition, the United States currency lost over 95% of its value. On top of this, cash was no longer risk-free; debt was.

And as a result of this, the cost of everything soared.

So the next time you find yourself asking, *"why is everything so expensive? I remember when I was younger this cost much less"*, you know the answer.

It's because the United States financial system is run by a Central Bank with no limits to its money printing.

Good. God. Almighty.

CHAPTER 2:
THE BUILDING OF A DEBT MOUNTAIN

To summate Chapter 1…

The United States Central Bank or Federal Reserve (the Fed) was created in 1913. From that point onwards, the Fed, not Congress, was in charge of printing the US dollar.

In 1933, then-President Franklin Delano Roosevelt confiscated Americans' gold. He then devalued the US dollar against gold by ~70%, erasing an entire generation's wealth, and initiating the process of breaking the US dollar's link to the precious metal.

President Richard Nixon completed this process in 1971, severing the US dollar from any remaining gold peg and ending the convertibility of US dollars and US debt into gold. From this point onward, there was technically no limit to the amount of debt the United States government could issue.

Why?

The United States would be paying all of its debts *exclusively* in US dollars… dollars that the Fed could print at anytime.

What followed was the creation of the largest mountain of debt in history. From 1971 onward, the United States' debts grew almost continuously.

Chart 6. US Public Debt, Trillions US Dollars (1970-2016).

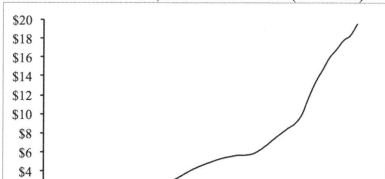

Note: Data adapted from Federal Reserve Bank of St. Louis (2017)[5]

I want to stress here that there isn't anything inherently wrong with debt. In fact, borrowing money can be a good thing if the borrowed money is put to use productively (invested in assets/projects that will generate economic growth).

The United States was at this stage for much of the 1970s as well as the early 1980s, with each new $1 in debt it issued producing nearly $1 in economic growth.

When taking on debt starts to become a problem is if the borrowed money is *not* invested productively. A country can get away with this for a while, but eventually the debt becomes a net drag on its economic output, as the country has to use more and more of its tax revenues to cover the debt's interest payments.

The United States has been transitioning to this phase since the mid-1980s, with each new $1 in debt issuance producing only $0.30 to $0.50 in economic growth. And, by the time the country hit the new millennium, each new $1 in debt issuance produced just $0.10 in economic growth.

You can see this in the rise in the United States' Debt to Gross Domestic Product or GDP ratio, which measures debt as a percentage of annual economic output. When a country's pace of debt growth exceeds its pace of economic growth, its Debt to GDP ratio rises.

This process began for the United States in 1981. Since that time, with few exceptions, the country's Debt to GDP ratio has been rising.

Chart 7. US Public Debt to Gross Domestic Product Ratio (1970-2016).

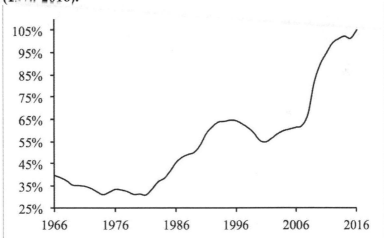

Note: Data adapted from Federal Reserve Bank of St. Louis (2017)[6]

Here's how it happened…

Politicians Promise, But Bonds Markets Deliver

Before moving forward, I want to stress that the following argument is not a left vs. right or, Democrat vs. Republican argument. This is simply an outline of how western-style democracies such as the United States currently function from a monetary standpoint.

The basic outline for any political campaign in a western-style democracy is as follows.

1. Candidate A campaigns on a platform of fixing various social or economic problems.
2. As far as the government is concerned, solving these problems involves spending money.
3. The money that the government uses to "solve" these problems is generated via tax revenues.
4. If tax revenues are not enough, the government issues debt.

In simple terms, government solutions to problems usually involve creating a government program.

The government finances these programs (as well as the rest of the federal budget) using tax revenues. If tax revenues are not great enough to cover all of these costs, the government runs a deficit.

That deficit is financed by the country issuing debt in the bond markets.

Here's how it works…

The following is a technical breakdown of how the United States issues debt. If you are not interested in these details and simply want to continue on to the big picture analysis of the United States' debt situation, skip ahead to the section titled *The Fed's Worst Nightmare.*

How the United States Issues Debt

When the United States goes to issue debt, the US Department of the Treasury issues US Government Bonds, also called Treasuries, via a process called a "bond auction."

The firms that participate in these auctions are called primary dealers. They make up the bulk of the buying during an auction and are responsible for insuring that the auction goes smoothly.

For instance, if enough outside investors don't show up to buy the Treasuries that are being issued, the primary dealers will step in to buy them thereby insuring there isn't a "failed auction."

In this sense, the primary dealers are at the top of the financial food chain.

Below is a list of the primary dealers as of late 2016. You'll immediately recognize them as the largest banks/ financial institutions in the world. These are the Too Big To Fail or TBTF firms. And, we'll be delving into their role in the financial system later in another chapter.

- Bank of Nova Scotia, New York Agency
- BMO Capital Markets Corp.
- BNP Paribas Securities Corp.
- Barclays Capital Inc.
- Cantor Fitzgerald & Co.
- Citigroup Global Markets Inc.
- Credit Suisse Securities (USA) LLC
- Daiwa Capital Markets America Inc.
- Deutsche Bank Securities Inc.
- Goldman, Sachs & Co.
- HSBC Securities (USA) Inc.
- Jefferies LLC
- J.P. Morgan Securities LLC
- Merrill Lynch, Pierce, Fenner & Smith Incorporated
- Mizuho Securities USA Inc.

- Morgan Stanley & Co. LLC
- Nomura Securities International, Inc.
- RBC Capital Markets, LLC
- RBS Securities Inc.
- Societe Generale, New York Branch
- TD Securities (USA) LLC
- UBS Securities LLC.
- Wells Fargo Securities, LLC

So, when a debt auction ends, *someone* (either an outside investor or a primary dealer) has purchased the debt.

Now, as I mentioned earlier, US Government Debt or Treasuries are the bedrock of the US financial system.

However, I want to be clear here. It's not as though the United States simply issues debt and then owes the lender money forever. The United States issues debt for specific periods of time, called maturation periods. So when I refer to "Treasuries," I am not merely referring to one thing: there are actually several different types of US Treasuries.

In broad terms, there are three categories: Treasury Bills or T-bills (usually short-term debt), Treasury Notes (long-term debt of up to 10 years), and Treasury Bonds (long-term debt for 20 or 30 years).

I've broken down all of the different maturation periods by category in the list below.

<u>Treasury Bill Maturation Periods:</u>
4 Weeks
13 Weeks
26 Weeks
52 Weeks

Treasury Note Maturation Periods:
2 Years
3 Years
5 Years
7 Years
10 Years

Treasury Bond Maturation Periods:
20 Years
30 Years

Obviously, this is a lot to wrap your head around. To make things even more complicated, the United States is continuously issuing debt in virtually all of these denominations either by issuing new debt or simply rolling over old debts that have come due (in this situation, investors choose to lend their capital to the United States again rather than have it returned and so the old bonds are simply "rolled over" into new ones).

However, out of the bunch, the 10-Year Treasury Note is the most important for assessing the United States financial system's risk profile.

This is because the average economic cycle is roughly 10 years: during any given 10-year period, the US economy is likely to experience both an upswing of growth and a contraction.

With that in mind, the yield on the 10-Year Treasury Note (the interest rate the United States government pays to lenders on the bond) is considered the "risk free rate of return" for the United States financial system.

You're probably asking, *"What is a bond yield or rate?"*

I don't want to get too technical here, as bond pricing is actually very complicated. So for simplicity's sake, when it comes to US Government Bonds or Treasuries there are three basic things you need to understand:

1) These bonds have a price (when first issued and trading at 100 cents on the dollar this is called "par value").

2) These bond prices are generally free-floating, meaning that the price can change depending on whether or not investors are feeling positive (bullish) or negative (bearish) about a particular bond's future value at any given time.

3) A bond's yield, or the interest payment the bond pays a lender, is based on its price. For example, a 2% yield on a $100 par value bond means the lender is being paid $2 per year (usually in semi-annual installments).

Let me give you a simple example.

Let's say the US government issues $1 billion worth of 10-Year US Treasuries at a par value of $100 and yielding 10%. You, along with many other investors (hedge funds, investment banks, even foreign governments), buy these bonds.

In your case, we'll say you bought just one bond. What this means is that you just loaned the US government $100 for 10 years (assuming you hold the bond to completion or "maturity").

In exchange for this, the US government is going to pay you $10 in interest per year (again the payment is usually broken into semi-annual installments so in this case it would be $5 every six months) until it finally pays you the full $100 back at the end of the 10-year period.

Now, you may decide you want to hold this bond the full ten years, but many investors will buy and sell bonds without ever waiting until the bond matures.

As a result of this, the bond is "free-floating" in the financial markets with various traders and investors buying and selling it based on their forecasts of future economic growth as well as the current rate of inflation and other factors.

This is what determines the price of the bond you are holding in your own portfolio.

Now, let's say that investors believe 10-Year Treasuries are a great investment in this current economic environment and start to buy them, pushing the price of the bond you own up from $100 to $120.

The bond is still yielding the same amount in dollar terms ($10), but now that yield is just 8.3% ($10/$120=8.3%).

Obviously, you'd be very happy in this context: you've just made $20 dollars on your $100 par value bond. That's a 20% return!

But do you know who is even happier than you are about 10-Year Treasury notes rallying this much?

The US government.

You see, when investors pushed the value of your bond up to $120, the yield on your bond fell to 8.3%. This was the market signaling that an 8.3% yield is an appropriate rate of return for lending money to the US government for 10 years.

Put another way, the US government can now issue new debt for 10 years and pay **out even less in interest to its lenders**. Borrowing money just got cheaper for Uncle Sam.

If this process continues for some time, 10-Year Treasuries are deemed to be in a "bull market" or a period in which their prices rise almost continuously (the term "bull" stems from the notion that the market is charging forward like a bull). Throughout a bull market in bonds, bond yields (the cost of servicing the debt, or the payouts the government has to pay to investors) continuously *fall*.

In the simplest of terms possible, during a bull market in bonds, **it becomes cheaper and cheaper for the borrower to issue debt.**

This is precisely what has happened in the United States since 1981.

Starting in 1981, US Treasury Notes entered a bull market. Throughout this time period, Treasury prices generally rose while yields fell.

What this means is that since 1981, it has been continuously cheaper and easier for the US government to issue debt (see Chart 8).

Chart 8. Yield on the 10-Year Treasury Note (1970-2016).

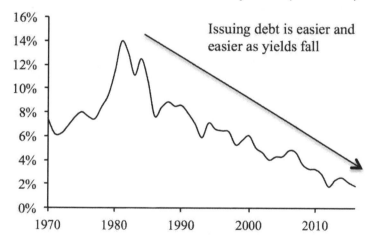

Note: Data adapted from Federal Reserve Bank of St. Louis (2017)[4]

Which is why around 1981, the United States' Debt to GDP ratio began rising. This was not a left vs. right or Democrat vs. Republican issue; this was a *"we can spend money we don't have with few, if any, consequences"* issue.

Regardless of which political party was in the White House or controlling Congress, starting in 1981, the United States' debt pile grew more quickly than its economy. Again, this is not a political argument; this is just human nature or what happens when acting a certain way no longer has any immediate, significantly negative consequences (see chart 9 below).

Chart 9. US Public Debt to Gross Domestic Product Ratio with Notes (1970-2016).

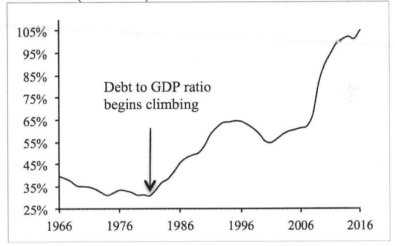

Note: Data adapted from Federal Reserve Bank of St. Louis (2017)[6]

We've just covered a lot of ground, so let's step back and take a big picture look at this.

1) In 1971, the US dollar was completely severed from any link to gold.

2) That same year, the US government decided it would only pay its debts in US dollars (US dollars that it could print anytime in any amount with little consequence since the US dollar was the reserve currency of the world).

3) In 1981, the United States bond market entered a bull market. From this point onward for 30+ years, it became continuously cheaper and easier for the US government to issue debt.

This is the environment in which debt mountains can be accrued.

Indeed, Uncle Sam wasn't the only one taking advantage of cheap rates to issue debt. Starting in 1981, everyone from state governments to municipalities, corporations, and even consumers began borrowing money (see Chart 10 below).

Chart 10. US State and Local Debt, US Corporate Debt, US Consumer Credit, Billions of US Dollars (1970-2016).

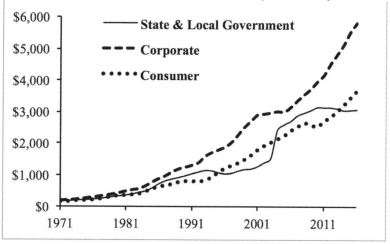

Note: Data adapted from Federal Reserve Bank of St. Louis (2017)[7]

All of this counts as debt in the financial system. So when we talk about the United States' Debt Mountain, we're not just talking about this (Chart 11)...

Chart 11. US Public Debt, Trillions US Dollars (1970-2016).

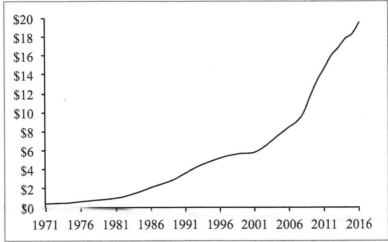

Note: Data adapted from Federal Reserve Bank of St. Louis (2017)[5]

… we're really talking about this (Chart 12).

Chart 12. Total US Debt Securities, Trillions US Dollars (1970-2016).

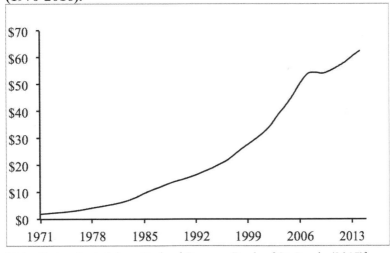

Note: Data adapted from Federal Reserve Bank of St. Louis (2017)[3]

It is generally believed that a Debt to GDP ratio of 100% means that a country is approaching bankrupty.

Well, based on the total debt in the system, the United States hit this level around 1984. And by the mid- to late- '90s, it was well over 250% (and I am not including unfunded liabilities such as Social Security or Medicare which are not counted in "official" debt numbers).

Put simply, since the mid-'80s, and most assuredly by the mid-'90s, the United States was at a point of "debt saturation": a point at which every segment of the economy was "maxed out" in terms of its debt load.

As a result of this, whenever a financial crisis erupted in the United States (or elsewhere with the potential to spill over into the United States) the Fed acted quickly to prop the system up to insure that the crisis didn't spread to the debt markets.

The reason for this was very simple…

In a world in which the entire United States financial system is saturated in debt, the single most important issue for its Central Bank to avoid is deflation.

What is deflation?

The "D" Word: The Fed's Worst Nightmare

You've probably heard the word "deflation" mentioned at some point by financial pundits on business TV. Usually, it's referred to in hushed tones as though it's some kind of unspeakable evil.

This is completely bogus.

Deflation is the process by which something falls in price. It is a perfectly normal development for a healthy economy. In fact, deflation is actually an intrinsic part of technological advancement (for instance, the cell phone you own today is both more sophisticated and cheaper than the original models from a decade ago).

DEBT deflation, on the other hand, is a completely different issue. And it absolutely terrifies Central Bankers like those running the Federal Reserve.

Debt deflation is the process by which *debt* falls in value.

Why does this matter? After all, any free-floating security can rise or fall anytime. The stock market routinely drops 5% and financial pundits say that *"stocks are now a bargain"* or *"it's time to buy!"*

With debt, a drop in price is a BIG deal because when bond prices fall, bond yields RISE. And a higher bond yield is indicative of **greater risk**.

If you'll recall our example of investing in 10-Year Treasuries from a few pages back… imagine if the 10-Year Treasury Note you bought at par value of $100 with a yield of 10% (meaning $10 in interest payments per year) suddenly fell in value to $80.

First off, you've just lost $20 or 20% of your initial investment. Obviously you'd be pretty upset.

But you know who'd be even more upset?

The US government.

Remember, yields don't change in dollar terms (Uncle Sam would still be paying you $10 in interest on your bond every year). However, because your bond is now worth only $80, the yield on the bond is now 12.5% ($10/$80= 12.5%).

This means the bond market is saying, *"lending money to the US government for 10 years is a LOT riskier than it was before."* As a result, going forward, when the US government wants to issue 10-Year Treasuries, it will have to do so at a higher yield.

Put simply, it is now MORE expensive for the US government to issue debt.

However, the risk of debt deflation goes even beyond that… Remember that US Government Debt is the supposed "risk free" rate for the financial system.

So, if it is now RISKIER to lend money to the US government, this will have a ripple effect for all other assets in the financial system. When this happens ALL bonds (municipal, corporate, etc.) will begin to adjust to this heightened state of risk.

This is systemic debt deflation… the process through which debt becomes MORE expensive to issue. And if it becomes bad enough, you enter a debt panic, at which point bond prices fall so much that the market is effectively saying, ***"GET OUT! You're not going to get your money back! The borrower is BROKE!"***

Eventually, default or restructuring (refinancing the debt, usually at a smaller amount with a lower yield) is the only option.

Systemically, debt deflation for the US Treasury Bond market would mean both a financial AND an economic collapse.

Why?

As debt deflation rippled throughout the financial system, riskier borrowers would begin to default.

By way of context, when I say "borrowers," I don't necessarily mean individual Americans: a borrower can be a massive corporation like IBM, or a municipality like the city of Charlotte.

- If the borrower happens to be a corporation, debt deflation would mean that financially the company is in serious trouble and will be laying off large numbers of its employees or resorting to other drastic measures to shore up its finances.

- If the borrower is a municipality like the city of New York, it means the city is going bust and a large-scale restructuring of its finances will follow (this usually features cutting things like pension payments, city services and other items).

- If the borrower is an entire country like the United States… then you're talking about systemic collapse similar to that of Argentina in 2001 or Greece in 2012.

In pictorial form, a major bout of debt deflation for the US financial system would look something like Chart 13.

Chart 13. Hypothetical Debt Deflation Crisis in Total US Debt Securities and Its Impact on US Gross Domestic Product, Trillions US Dollars

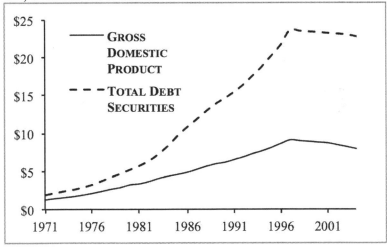

Note: Proprietary graph based on projections using data available at Federal Reserve Bank of St. Louis (2017)

Bear in mind, we are talking about hypotheticals here. Perhaps Chart 13 doesn't seem like a big deal to you, so let's consider a real world example of debt deflation.

Remember the 2008 crisis? Remember how it felt? Remember how people were acting as though the world was ending?

Well that "end of the world" collapse was barely a blip of debt deflation for the mountain of debt that existed in the US financial system at the time (see Chart 14).

Chart 14. Debt Deflation of the 2008 Crisis in Total US Debt Securities and Its Impact on US Gross Domestic Product, Trillions US Dollars (1945-2016)

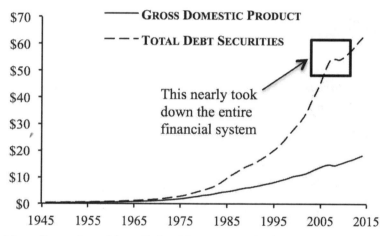

Note: Data adapted from Federal Reserve Bank of St. Louis (2017)[3]

If 2008 was that blip, imagine what it would feel like for the United States' debt bubble to deflate to the point that debt levels were within spitting distance of US Gross Domestic Product again (as they were from 1946 until 1985).

This would be a financial crisis many magnitudes worse than 2008.

We're talking about another Great Depression coupled with a financial systemic reset (think most major banks go out of business, many large publicly traded corporations default on their debts, and millions of American consumers lose access to credit).

This situation has been the single biggest fear for the Federal Reserve ever since the United States reached the point at which debt deflation was a systemic issue (somewhere in the early to mid-1990s).

Put simply, by the time the United States' Debt Mountain reached this stage (Chart 15)...

Chart 15. Total US Debt Securities and US Gross Domestic Product, Trillions US Dollars (1971-1999).

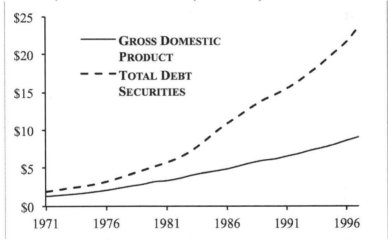

Note: Data adapted from Federal Reserve Bank of St. Louis (2017)[3]

... the Fed was concerned with one thing only: **stopping debt deflation from ever spreading into the US Treasury market.**

For this reason, starting in the late '90s, whenever a major asset class began to suffer a bout of deflation, the Federal Reserve quickly dealt with it by creating a financial bubble in an alternate asset class.

Consider the following…

From 1996 to 2000, the Unites States experienced a bubble in tech stocks called the Tech Bubble (we will delve into this in our next chapter). When this bubble burst, it resulted in the Tech Crash of 2000-2001 during which time stocks plunged over 50%.

The Fed dealt with this by creating another bubble, this time in housing/ real estate.

This was <u>intentional</u>.

When the Housing Bubble burst in late 2006/ early 2007, parts of the US financial system experienced debt deflation culminating in the 2008 Crash. The Fed dealt with this by creating a bubble in US sovereign bonds or Treasuries from 2009 until today.

And because Treasuries are the ultimate backstop/ measure of risk for the financial system, the current Bond Bubble is in fact an **Everything Bubble** (a term we coined in 2014).

We're going to be covering each of these developments in the next few chapters. However, before moving forward we first need to define the term "financial bubble."

What is a Bubble and How Does It Happen?

First and foremost, you need to know that asset bubbles are nothing new.

Human beings are irrational. And that irrationality lends itself to greed-induced manias, particularly when an investment has the potential to let investors, *"get rich quickly."*

Before you start arguing with this, consider that Isaac Newton, the father of Calculus and possibly one of the most intelligent/ rational people in history, got caught up in an investment craze and lost the equivalent of ~$2 million in today's money, leading to him stating, *"I can calculate the motions of heavenly bodies, but not the madness of people."*

Unless you've invented an entire field of mathematics, and can project the order of the cosmos well into the future, odds are you're not smarter than Newton and no less susceptible to greed or other human foibles.

With that in mind, asset bubbles have been a regular feature of the global economy since at least the early 1600s. To date, there have been bubbles in tulips, companies with dibs on the gold and silver reserves of the "New World," Japanese real estate, US technology companies, and more.

So what is a bubble?

The NASDAQ website offers the following definition of a bubble:

> A market phenomenon characterized by surges in asset prices to levels significantly above the fundamental value of that asset. Bubbles are often hard to detect in real time because there is disagreement over the fundamental value of the asset.
>
> Source: NASDAQ Financial Glossary[8]

The first part of this definition (the part about surging asset prices) is accurate: bubbles are asset manias or periods of time in which an asset surges higher in price.

The second part of this definition (the one about bubbles being hard to identify) is something of a cop out. *Some* asset bubbles are hard to identify. Others are plainly obvious.

Indeed, I would argue that there are in fact two types of financial asset bubbles.

1) Bubbles driven by investment manias surrounding a new technology, particularly when the future economic impact/ value of the technology is difficult to value (for example, the bubble in technology stocks during the late '90s). **These are the bubbles that are <u>difficult</u> to identify in real-time.**

2) Bubbles that are induced by aggressive credit expansions by Central Banks, resulting in various asset classes moving to levels that are multiple standard deviations away from their historic relationships to important related economic fundamentals (for example, the bubble in US real estate during the mid-'00s). **These are the bubbles that are easy to identify in real-time.**

The distinction seems pretty obvious. However, this distinction is one that the financial elites, particularly the Federal Reserve, don't want to make or admit, especially in public.

Why?

Remember from Chapter 1, the Fed was originally created to maintain financial stability and to mitigate financial crises (whether it has achieved this is debatable).

For this reason, Federal Reserve leadership cannot accept either of my two definitions of a bubble because doing so would either reveal that the Fed is actually clueless about some of the most important economic developments (definition #1) or is directly responsible for creating asset bubbles (definition #2).

Put simply, if your job is to maintain confidence in the financial system, the last thing you're going to do is proclaim your ignorance or culpability in financial disasters (all bubbles end in disaster).

Instead, you're going to maintain an air of *"knowing everything"* while debating whether or not bubbles exist based on various nebulous concepts such as *"what is the fundamental value of a given asset?"*

Indeed, this was the very aura maintained by former Fed Chairman Alan Greenspan during his 19-year tenure as he ushered the United States into its current era of serial bubbles.

With that in mind, Greenspan belongs in the same category as Franklin Delano Roosevelt and Richard Nixon as a key historical figure who permitted the financial system to become the massive debt-fueled mess that it is today.

If you recall from Chapter 1...

Franklin Delano Roosevelt confiscated Americans' private property (gold) then devalued their savings by ~70%. He also began severing the link between gold and the US dollar (the so-called Gold Standard). The US dollar lost 69% of its purchasing power in the decades following this.

Richard Nixon finished the job Roosevelt started, severing the link between gold and the US dollar completely. Nixon also passed legislation stating that the US would pay its debts solely using US dollars. This allowed the US to grow its debt exponentially as all debts would be paid back using dollars that the Fed could print at any time. The US dollar lost another 84% in purchasing power following this.

Put simply, Roosevelt and Nixon severed the US dollar from gold, opening the door to endless money printing.

Former Fed Chairman Alan Greenspan was the man who walked through this metaphoric door in 1987 and actually hit the "print" button on the United States' money press.

He then held it there non-stop for nearly 20 years, growing the US Debt Mountain to stratospheric levels and bringing about the era of "Serial Bubbles": the era in which the Fed began to *intentionally* create asset bubbles as part of its monetary policy.

Good. God. Almighty.

CHAPTER 3:
THE ERA OF SERIAL BUBBLES BEGINS

Do you know who Alan Greenspan is?

You might have heard his name before. You might even have a sense that he is involved in finance in some way.

What you might not know is that the entire financial mess of the last 20 years could justly be laid at Greenspan's feet.

Alan Greenspan served as Chairman of the Federal Reserve from 1987 to 2006. In that capacity, he was in charge of US monetary policy, as well as regulating Wall Street, for nearly 20 years.

Throughout that time, the official narrative was that Greenspan was a genius who manufactured an economic paradise in which the US economy continually grew with only minor contractions as opposed to serious recessions.

More importantly for Wall Street and the financial media that writes about markets, Greenspan was believed to be responsible for creating one of the greatest bull markets in stock market history.

If Greenspan was an economic genius for the US public, he was a virtual god for the financial industry.

If you think I'm being facetious, consider a few headlines from Greenspan's tenure as Fed Chairman...

Why Greenspan Is Bullish

~Fortune Magazine, 1987.

In Greenspan We Trust: The Powerful Fed Chairman Is Headed For Four More Years, To the Relief of Corporate America. What Does It Mean? Simply This: No Recession. No Inflation. No Voodoo.

~Fortune Magazine, 1996.

Why is This Man Smiling? How Alan Greenspan Views- and Soothes- the Economy

~Time 1997

Alan Greenspan Comes To The Party

~Forbes, 2000

A Cheer for Greenspan, the Full-Employment Chairman

~ *Barron's*, 2000

Greenspan: Our economic czar for life
~Chicago Tribune, 2003

As you can see, Greenspan was virtually worshipped for much of his tenure at the Fed. Indeed, at one point "the Maestro" as he was called, was considered to be such an economic titan that journalists penned pieces about how to invest based on his *facial expressions* during congressional testimony.

What's extraordinary is that this slavish praise didn't end even after a major financial catastrophe occurred during Greenspan's watch (the Tech Crash of 2000-2001, which we will detail shortly). In 2001, the media even suggested that the President of the United States (George W. Bush) was *courting* Greenspan to remain as Fed Chairman.

Feud? What Feud? W. Presents The Courtship of Alan Greenspan

~Fortune, 2001.

Again, the financial media hailed Greenspan as an economic god.

However, Greenspan was no god. The reality is that he was a mediocre economist and an even worse regulator who "signed off" on the largest debt expansion in US history (at the time): a period in which the slope of the US Debt Mountain went parabolic.

By the time Greenspan stepped down as Fed chair in 2006, the United States was completely saturated with debt to the point that even a whiff of debt deflation put the entire financial system at risk.

Lest you think I am being harsh here, let me show you the following.

When Greenspan took over the Fed, the US Debt Mountain was at this stage (Chart 16).

Chart 16. Total US Debt Securities and US Gross Domestic Product, Trillions US Dollars (1971-1987).

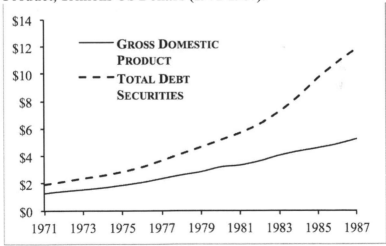

Note: Data adapted from Federal Reserve Bank of St. Louis (2017)[3]

A child with a ruler could see that the Unites States' debt growth was beginning to rapidly outpace its economic growth. And, it's not like you can argue that Greenspan was ignorant of the fact that this was happening (the data I used to make Chart 16 **comes from one of the Fed's own websites).**

Greenspan let that situation become this (Chart 17).

Chart 17. Total US Debt Securities and US Gross Domestic Product, Trillions US Dollars (1971-2006).

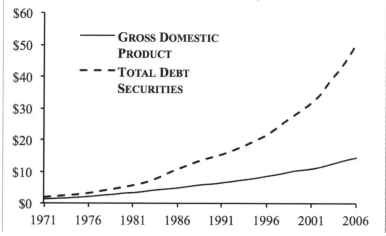

Note: Data adapted from Federal Reserve Bank of St. Louis (2017)[3]

This was Greenspan's TRUE legacy.

The "economic paradise" of continuous growth was in fact just a situation in which each and every economic concern was met with more money printing and more debt. As a result of this, for nearly 20 years, the entire United States (from the United States as a country down to individual Americans) continued to borrow money cheaply to buy/fund things it couldn't afford.

In numeric terms, Greenspan permitted the US Debt Mountain to quadruple in size. By the time he was done, the United States' total Debt to GDP ratio was 323%, making it **a systemic issue.**

Now, obviously, you cannot claim that ALL of this was Greenspan's fault (Congress, the banks, and even individual Americans played their parts in this tragedy).

However, what you *can* say without any doubt is that as Fed Chairman throughout this period, Greenspan was the chief regulator for the US financial system. **As such, it was his job to maintain financial stability (remember, the Fed's primary mandate, indeed, the entire "official" reason the Fed was created, was to maintain <u>financial stability</u>).**

From a metaphoric perspective, Greenspan was like a university campus cop whose job is to shut down college parties when they begin to get out of hand: he can't stop undergrads from *starting* a party or drinking, but he *can* show up and close the party down before real trouble starts.

Greenspan didn't do this. Instead, he routinely ignored excessive risk-taking "parties," pretending they weren't even happening despite clear evidence they were.

The campus cop metaphor is a good one, but to fully understand how the Fed is meant to "police" the economy, you need to understand the Fed's "dual mandate" as well as how it controls risk-taking (the equivalent of "parties" in our campus cop metaphor) in the financial system via interest rates.

The following is a technical outline of the Fed's responsibilities and operations. If you're not interested in these details, feel free to skip ahead to the section titled *Greenspan's True Legacy.*

The Fed's "Dual Mandate"

If you recall from Chapter 1, the Federal Reserve banking system was originally designed to insure another 1907-type financial crisis <u>didn't</u> happen again.

By quick way of review, that crisis was caused by unregulated banks, called "trusts", making excessive loans (meaning they didn't have enough capital on hand to stay in business if their borrowers began defaulting).

To stop a repeat of this mess, once the Federal Reserve banking system was created, every bank that was granted a federal charter to operate in the United States was REQUIRED to join it.

The idea here was that in this fashion all federally chartered banks would have access to additional capital through the Fed should another banking crisis hit.

From 1913 when the Fed was created until the 1970s, this was the Fed's primary focus: **maintaining financial stability.**

However, once former President Richard Nixon took the US dollar off the Gold Standard completely in 1971, a new type of crisis occurred: a crisis of inflation.

If you're not familiar with the concept of inflation, it's essentially a period of time in which the cost of everything rises dramatically (put another way, the purchasing power of the US dollar collapses).

Remember Chart 1 (the chart in Chapter 1 showing the decline in purchasing power of the US Dollar from 1913 onwards)? That chart represents the long-term effect of *gradual* inflation.

However, in the 1970s, the United States experienced a period of *accelerated* inflation in which prices rose **across the board by as much as 15% in the span of a few years** (see Chart 18).

Chart 18. Year Over Year Change in Rate of US Inflation (1960 to 1990).

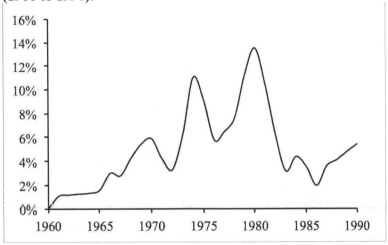

Note: Data adapted from Federal Reserve Bank of St. Louis (2017)[4]

To make matters worse, the US economy contracted sharply over the same time period. So you had a collapsing economy, with people losing their jobs, occurring at the same time that the cost of living was soaring.

Nowadays, we're used to our cost of living rising even during periods of economic weakness. But before the 1970s, this was considered **impossible** (remember, up until that point the US dollar was still linked to gold and so inflation, while gradual, was generally kept under control).

Because it was believed that you couldn't have inflation AND a collapsing economy simultaneously, the Fed was never *explicitly* tasked with managing these issues.

The inflationary recession of the 1970s changed this. As a result, in 1977, the *Federal Reserve Act* (the official legislation that granted the Fed its powers) was amended to state that the Fed was to...

"… maintain long run growth of the monetary and credit aggregates commensurate with the economy's long run potential to increase production, so as to promote effectively **the goals of maximum employment, stable prices and moderate long-term interest rates."** [emphasis added]

Source: Federal Reserve Act[9]

This is the Fed's so-called "dual mandate": to maintain a strong economy/maximum employment *while* keeping inflation under control via interest rates.

We'll now discuss how the Fed is meant to do it.

How the Fed Controls the "Cost" of Money

As part of its regulatory powers, the Federal Reserve banking system requires ALL federally chartered US banks (banks granted charters to operate nationwide in the United States) to deposit a certain amount of capital with a Federal Reserve Bank as a kind of buffer against liquidity crises.

This is why when the Fed Banking System was created, it was set up with 12 different Federal Reserve Banks throughout the United States. Those branches are in Boston, New York, Philadelphia, Cleveland, Richmond, Atlanta, Chicago, St. Louis, Minneapolis, Kansas City, Dallas, and San Francisco.

In this manner every bank in the United States, regardless of its location, has a Federal Reserve Bank in relatively close proximity.

The deposits a bank keeps with a Federal Reserve Bank are called "**Federal Funds**" and are based on the size of each individual bank's loan portfolio (its total assets vs. total liabilities) on any given day.

Typically, a given bank's Federal Funds are meant to equal ~10% of that bank's Demand Accounts (think of checking or savings accounts from which you can *demand* your money back).

Now, some banks might happen to have excess capital lying around (perhaps they haven't generated many loans recently). The Fed permits these banks to *lend* their extra capital to other banks in the system.

The interest rate charged on these loans is called the **Fed's Target Federal Funds Rate.**

<u>This is considered the "cost of money" in the financial system. It is the price at which money flows from one entity to another. It is also the interest rate the Fed "controls."</u>

When you hear the news that the Fed "cut rates" or "raised rates," it's not referring to an actual physical rate that the Fed raises or lowers. Instead, it's referring to the *targeted* rate that the Fed aims for when it determines how much one bank might charge another for extra capital.

Let's say that the Fed's Target Federal Fed Fund Rate is 0.50% to 1.00%. This means that as long as banks are lending capital to each other at rates somewhere in this spectrum, the Fed is fine with it.

However, let's say that banks start lending money to each other at rates outside this range, for example, 1.25%. This indicates that the cost of money in the system is getting more "<u>expensive</u>."

The Fed will step in at this time and start buying securities from the banking system. The Fed usually purchases Treasuries via its New York branch which is responsible for market operations (more on this in the next chapter).

When the Fed does this, it is taking assets out of the system (onto the Fed's balance sheet) and putting more money into it. This *increases* the base money supply in the financial system, forcing rates to go lower (there is more money, so money "costs" less).

The same process works in reverse.

Let's say that the Fed's Target Federal Funds Rate is between 0.50% and 1.00% and the Fed observes that banks are lending money to one another for only 0.3%. This means money is too "cheap," based on where the Fed wants rates to be.

So the Fed steps in and starting selling securities that it owns (the Fed maintains a balance sheet of many securities at any given time).

When it sells securities, the Fed is putting assets into the financial system and taking money out. This reduces the amount of base money circulating in the financial system, causing rates to rise, which makes money more "expensive."

This is how the Fed controls interest rates. Again, there is no exact rate the Fed controls; instead the New York branch of the Fed simply buys or sells securities to insure that the Effective Federal Funds Rate (the actual rate banks charge one another) is somewhere in the range of the Fed's Target Federal Funds Rate.

To return to the Fed's dual mandate: "the goal of the Fed is to maintain economic growth/full employment without letting inflation get out of control."

The Fed's Target Federal Funds is meant to be the primary tool through which the Fed accomplishes this. If inflation begins to accelerate, the Fed is meant to RAISE the Target Federal Funds rate (make money more expensive) in order to stop it.

Unfortunately, in the past, any Fed Chair who did this was committing career suicide.

Remember, once the United States abandoned the Gold Standard completely and began ballooning its debts, any time the Fed raised rates significantly it made borrowing more expensive and ran the risk of triggering debt deflation.

Put simply, once the US economy was completely addicted to debt, any time issuing debt began to grow more expensive for the financial system, there were political consequences.

Paul Volcker, who served as Fed Chairman during the period of high inflation in the '70s and '80s, experienced precisely this.

To stop the rise of inflation, Volcker was forced to raise the Fed's Target Federal Funds Rate to the sky-high rate of 15%.

Unfortunately for him, this forced highly indebted farmers and other politically significant groups to go broke (imagine trying to pay a loan that is charging you 15% per year).

In fact, at one point during Volcker's tenure as Fed Chair, farmers actually drove their tractors to Washington DC and circled the Fed's headquarters.

Volcker left the Fed in 1987 and was replaced by Alan Greenspan, who was much more "career-focused."

From that point onwards, it was *Greenspan's* responsibility to maintain financial stability and pursue a policy of maximum economic growth without allowing inflation to get out of control.

In pictorial form, Greenspan's job, was to see Chart 19 taking place...

Chart 19. Total US Debt Securities and US Gross Domestic Product, Trillions US Dollars (1971-2006).

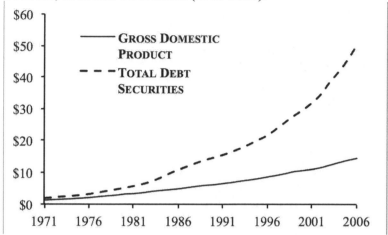

Note: Data adapted from Federal Reserve Bank of St. Louis (2017)[3]

… and do the equivalent of Chart 20...

Chart 20. Illustration of Hypothetical Fed Move to Raise Rates to Slow the Pace of US Debt Security Growth.

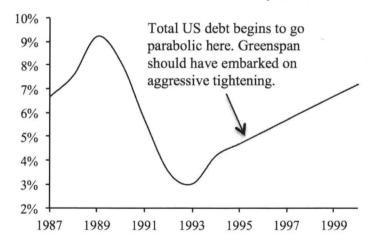

Note: Proprietary graph based on projections using data available at Federal Reserve Bank of St. Louis (2017)

… to stop it, or at least slow it down.

Greenspan didn't do that.

Instead of raising rates to halt the debt expansion, Greenspan maintained a policy of purposely keeping rates too low (more on this shortly). **As a result of this, the United States' Debt Mountain reach levels that were _systematically dangerous_.**

This is why Greenspan belongs in the same category as Franklin Delano Roosevelt and Richard Nixon as a key historical figure who permitted the financial system to become the massive bubble-driven mess that it is today.

All three men let short-term considerations and their own careerism blind them to the long-term implications of their policies. But whereas Roosevelt's or Nixon's decisions occurred in a short-time frame (in both cases their actions only required signing a single piece of legislation), Greenspan maintained his blunder for a **solid 19 years.**

As a result of this, he brought the United States to our current era of Serial Bubbles in which the Fed is forced to continuously and _intentionally_ create bubbles in order to stop debt deflation from taking down the financial system.

I want to stress just how incredible this is…

Greenspan's True Legacy: Bubbles On Top of More Bubbles

Between 1929 and 1987, the US was effectively asset bubble free.

Stocks, bonds, commodities, real estate, virtually any asset class you can name, had a roughly 60-year period during which their prices never reached levels that were obscenely disconnected

73

from underlying economic realities.

Along came Greenspan, and within the span of 16 years, the US had three **1-in-100 year asset bubbles.**

Under Greenspan's Fed:

1) The US stock market experienced its largest bubble in history (the Technology Stock Bubble or Tech Bubble): a bubble so massive that it made the previous largest bubble (1926-1929) look like a small bump.

2) The US housing market experienced its single largest bubble in 100 years: a bubble in which home prices rose **THREE STANDARD DEVIATIONS** above their historic relationship to incomes.

3) Wall Street created over $1 QUADRILLION in derivatives (yes, $1 QUADRILLION), resulting in an issue that Greenspan himself admitted would "implode" the financial system (we'll get to this next chapter).

Put simply, Greenspan presided over three "1-in-100 year" catastrophes in various asset classes.

This was his true legacy.

Remember my categorization of bubbles from last chapter, namely that there are in fact *two* types of asset price bubbles:

1) Bubbles driven by investment manias surrounding a new technology, particularly when the future economic impact/ value of the technology is difficult to value (for example, the bubble in technology stocks during the late '90s). **These are the bubbles that are difficult to identify in real-time.**

2) Bubbles that are induced by aggressive credit expansions by Central Banks, resulting in various asset classes moving to levels that are multiple standard deviations away from their historic relationships to important related economic fundamentals (for example, the bubble in US real estate during the mid-'00s). **These are the bubbles that are easy to identify in real-time.**

Greenspan oversaw <u>both</u> types of bubbles.

It would be bad enough if his mistakes were all in the first category (incompetence is a terrible trait for a Central Banker, especially the one in charge of the largest economy and reserve currency for the world).

Unfortunately, *at best,* you can argue that the first of Greenspan's bubbles (the Technology Stock Bubble) belongs in category #1. We know **for a fact** that the Housing Bubble and the Derivatives Bubble were issues that Greenspan *intentionally* ignored.

Let's dive in.

The Tech Bubble: Greenspan's "Mulligan"

Alan Greenspan's first bubble concerned the bubble in technology stocks that lasted from 1994 until 2000.

This is commonly referred to as the "Tech Bubble."

For those of you who are unfamiliar with this period in time, the Tech Bubble was a period of about six years (from 1994 to 2000) in which the stock market, particularly prices of technology companies, rose to extreme heights based on the perceived "growth" that the Internet would have on the economy.

We'll get into all of this shortly, but the key item I want you to be aware of is the fact that the consensus view of the Tech Bubble is that it was due solely to a breakthrough in technology.

This is misguided.

At *best,* you could argue that the Tech Bubble was *mainly* due to a major breakthrough in technology (the Internet) the future economic value of which was difficult to value.

At *worst,* a case could be made that Alan Greenspan willfully turned a blind eye to OBVIOUS issues in the financial system, allowing the Tech Bubble to go from a normal stock mania to a "1-in-100 year event."

For this reason, the Tech Bubble could perhaps be seen as "Greenspan's Mulligan" (a mulligan is a golf term for a mistake that you don't count on your score card).

The Technology Side of the Tech Bubble

The Internet is widely believed to have been created in the 1990s. However, the fact is that the first version of this technology had been around since the 1960s: the initial version, developed by the Department of Defense, consisted of a network that allowed multiple computers to connect to one another.

This technology went through several generations in development until the mid-'90s when the Internet officially went into commercial use via web browsers. From this point onwards, anyone with a computer and a phone jack could access the World Wide Web.

It was hailed as the single greatest technological breakthrough since the railroad: a technology that could potentially connect the entire world.

This was the "hard to value" part of the Tech Bubble: a completely new breakthrough in technology that opened the door to new sources of growth such as e-commerce. From a purely technical perspective, **the Internet meant you could now sell just about anything to anyone anywhere in the world.**

No one knew how to quantify this. After all, if you could *technically* sell to anyone in the world... does that mean that your potential market is now the entire world?

This is the kind of "hard to value" opportunity from which stock manias are made.

However, what *wasn't* difficult to see was that as early as 1996 things were clearly getting out of control in the stock market.

The Money Side of the Tech Bubble: Greenspan's Folly

The fact is that the Tech bubble *was* unusual even by tech mania standards.

First of all, the United States had experienced several technology revolutions prior to the creation of the Internet, none of which resulted in stock market bubbles like the one in the mid- to late-'90s.

Indeed, one could easily argue that the Personal Computer or PC Revolution of the late '70s and early '80s was of greater economic significance than the creation of the Internet... and yet that technological breakthrough never resulted in tech stocks going parabolic as they did during the late '90s Internet craze

During the PC revolution, the NASDAQ, or Technology Stock Market Index rose 342% over the course of 10 years (see Chart 21).

Chart 21. NASDAQ Composite Index (1976-1987).

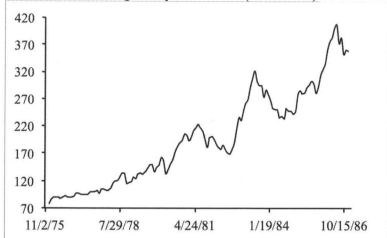

Note: Data adapted from NASDAQ OMX Group, Inc (2017)[10]

By way of contrast, during the 10 years of the Internet Tech Bubble from 1990 to 2000, the NASDAQ rose 960%. Look at Chart #22 and tell me that if you were Fed Chairman you couldn't see what was happening here.

Chart 22. NASDAQ Composite Index (1990-2000).

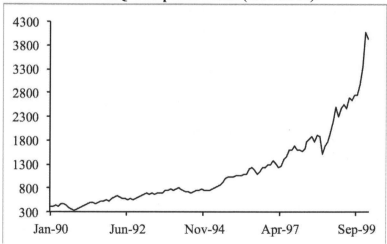

Note: Data adapted from NASDAQ OMX Group, Inc (2017)[10]

Even if the first six years from 1990 to 1996 were following the trajectory of a normal stock mania, the period from 1998 to 2000 was absolutely bonkers.

And yet, throughout this time period Alan Greenspan claimed **he couldn't tell that there was a bubble.**

On December 5, 1996, when the NASDAQ had already risen by an average of 60% for five years straight (a pace that would easily qualify as a "mania") Alan Greenspan gave his now famous speech in which he commented that asset values (read: stocks) were experiencing *"irrational exuberance."*

Here's the key quote (If you have trouble getting through it, I don't blame you... Greenspan seemed to take great pride in rambling forever without saying much):

> *Clearly, sustained low inflation implies less uncertainty about the future, and lower risk premiums imply higher prices of stocks and other earning assets. We can see that in the inverse relationship exhibited by price/earnings ratios and the rate of inflation in the past. **But how do we know when irrational exuberance has unduly escalated asset values**, which then become subject to unexpected and prolonged contractions as they have in Japan over the past decade? And how do we factor that assessment into monetary policy? **We as central bankers need not be concerned if a collapsing financial asset bubble does not threaten to impair the real economy, its production, jobs, and price stability.** Indeed, the sharp stock market break of 1987 had few negative consequences for the economy. But we should not underestimate or become complacent about the complexity of the interactions of asset markets and the economy. Thus, evaluating shifts in balance sheets generally, and in asset prices particularly, must be an integral part of the development of monetary policy. [emphasis added]*

-Alan Greenspan, December 5, 1996, American Enterprise Institute For Public Policy.

In laymen's terms Greenspan was saying, *"how can Central Bankers know when there's a bubble? Who knows?!? But, as long as the bubble doesn't hurt the economy when it implodes, everything is fine."*

I realize that all of this is a bit dense. So, let's return to our "campus cop" metaphor from earlier this chapter.

For Fed Chair Alan Greenspan to have this *"aw shucks, how can you tell?"* attitude about stock prices on December 5, 1996, would be like a campus cop watching a completely inebriated college student get behind the wheel of a car, and instead of stopping the kid from driving, simply turning to his partner and stating, *"that kid drank a lot of alcohol... but, was it so much alcohol for he cannot drive safely? That's quite the conundrum. Just how much is too much alcohol?!? Hmmmm."*

Meanwhile a car wreck is taking place.

Wall Street took Greenspan's speech in 1996 as a signal that the Fed wasn't going to do anything to halt the mania. So, Wall Street did what Wall Street does best: it went bananas taking almost *any company* public that had the terms "com" or "tech" in its name.

In 1996, the year in which Greenspan made this speech, 41% of the companies Wall Street took public (meaning they became publicly traded stocks) were unprofitable. Over the next two years, the percentage would nearly double to 80%. Over the same time period the NASDAQ QUADRUPLED.

Alan Greenspan *let* this happen. And when I say, "let," I mean it in a *literal* sense.

Remember the Fed's original purpose was "to maintain financial stability." And its Dual Mandate, established in 1977, was "to maintain economic growth *while* keeping inflation under control via interest rates."

With that in mind, consider that during the mid-'90s the US economy was growing at a roaring pace of 5%-6% per year, inflation was subdued, and yet Alan Greenspan was ***cutting*** interest rates or making money *cheaper.*

This is astonishing. Even more astounding is the fact that Greenspan was cutting rates during a period in which he acknowledged that the stock market was exhibiting "irrational exuberance." He literally knew things were beginning to get out of control.

You can see the impact of this policy on stocks. As soon as Greenspan started cutting rates, the NASDAQ began to go absolutely parabolic (see Chart 23)

Chart 23. NASDAQ Composite Index and Effective Federal Funds Rate (1995-2000).

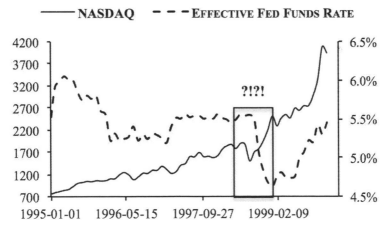

Note: Data adapted from NASDAQ OMX Group, Inc and Federal Reserve Bank of St. Louis (2017)[10,11]

To return to our "campus cop" metaphor, if Greenspan's "irrational exuberance" speech of 1996 was the equivalent of a campus cop letting a college student drive drunk, his decision to cut rates in 1998 was the equivalent of the cop getting the drunken kid out of the car only to force him to drink another three shots **before putting him back in the car and letting him drive away.**

It was complete and utter negligence. Anyone could see what was happening (again, the data I used to make Charts 22 and 23 comes from one of the Fed's <u>own websites</u>).

And yet, Greenspan continued to deny that the stock market was in a bubble. Indeed, as late as 1999, Greenspan claimed the following:

> *But bubbles generally are perceptible only after the fact. To spot a bubble in advance requires a judgment that hundreds of thousands of informed investors have it all wrong. Betting against markets is usually precarious at best.*

> - Alan Greenspan, June 17, 1999, US Congress.

This is why I have a hard time giving Greenspan a "mulligan" for his incompetence in dealing with the Tech Bubble. He had access to plenty of information that would have made it *obvious* that things were rapidly spinning out of control.

And yet he chose to do nothing. Actually, scratch that, he chose to make things worse.

Indeed, if the Tech Bubble was an egregious example of Fed incompetence, it paled in comparison to what was to follow.

The Tech Bubble burst (as all bubbles do) in 2000. When it was all said and done, over $6 trillion in wealth was wiped out.

By this point the US debt mountain had already gone completely parabolic to the point that if the debt markets got even a "whiff" of debt deflation, it would rapidly become a systemic issue. This represented the Fed's worst nightmare. And Alan Greenspan knew it.

Greenspan had a choice, *"do I go down in history as the guy who let the system implode, kicking off another Great Depression... or, do I reflate the system with another bubble and pass this mess off to the next guy?"*

Greenspan chose the second option. And he also chose "the next guy"... a Princeton Economics Professor by the name of Ben Bernanke.

And, so the Fed crossed the Financial Rubicon from allowing asset bubbles to occur to actively creating them on purpose.

Good. God. Almighty.

CHAPTER 4:

THE FED CROSSES THE FINANCIAL RUBICON

To recap the last chapter...

Alan Greenspan served as Fed Chair from 1987 until 2006.

During that time, Greenspan was in charge of maintaining stability in the US financial system, while also obeying the Fed's Dual Mandate of seeking maximum employment while keeping inflation at bay.

Instead of doing this, Greenspan turned a blind eye to obvious risks, particularly the sharp rise in US debt relative to the US economy, allowing the United States' debt mountain to become a systemic issue.

Greenspan *also* ignored the burgeoning bubble in Technology Stocks, cutting interest rates and making money even cheaper at a time when the US economy and inflation didn't warrant the move.

As a result of this, the Tech Bubble of the mid- to late-'90s became a 1-in-100-year event, the single largest stock bubble in history. And, when it burst as all stock bubbles do, Greenspan became terrified of debt deflation hitting the US financial system.

Again, in pictorial form, Greenspan was terrified of Chart 24...

Chart 24. Total US Debt Securities and US Gross Domestic Product, Trillions US Dollars (1946-2000).

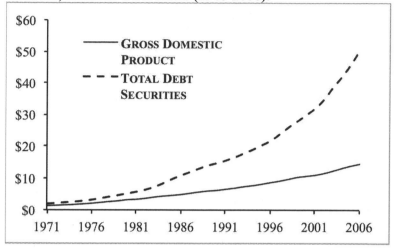

Note: Data adapted from Federal Reserve Bank of St. Louis (2017)[3]

... becoming Chart 25:

Chart 25. Illustration of Hypothetical Debt Deflation Crisis in Total US Debt Securities and Its Impact on US Gross Domestic Product, Trillions US Dollars.

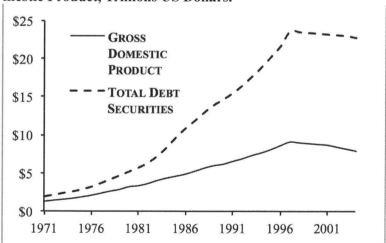

Note: Proprietary graph based on projections using data available at

So in 2002, Greenspan hired a college professor with zero experience in banking or business to be his primary advisor for dealing with the debt bubble.

That college professor was Ben Bernanke.

Who is Ben Bernanke?

Bernanke was an economics professor at Princeton University who was considered an expert on The Great Depression. His view, like Greenspan's, was that debt deflation was the cause of the Great Depression.

However, unlike Greenspan, Bernanke was convinced that the Fed could stop deflation from spreading. In fact, he was so convinced that he could stop it from happening again that he titled one of his first major speeches as a Fed Governor:

Deflation: Making Sure "It" Doesn't Happen Here

Note that Bernanke chose to put quotations around the word "it" as though deflation were some unspeakable evil. Also, note that he chose to use the grammatically incorrect "here" rather than the more accurate, time-centric term "now," (the speech was given in 2002 at a time when asset prices were indeed *deflating* as the Tech Bubble collapsed).

I emphasize this because I want to point out just how *terrified* the Fed was about the potential for debt deflation during the Tech Crash of the early 2000s.

On the surface, the Fed attempted to maintain an air of calm indifference. At a time when the Tech Crash had erased 72% of the NASDAQ's value in 12 months, Alan Greenspan referred to the issue as equity prices having *"contracted significantly"*.

87

However, behind this air of calmness, the Fed was terrified of debt deflation, hence Bernanke's hire and his immediate *"line in the sand"* talk of being able to stop deflation from occurring.

After all, you don't want people to stop focusing on the relatively insignificant Tech Bubble that just burst, and start focusing on the fact that the entire financial system is just a few months away from being totally insolvent, do you?

With Bernanke's guidance, then-Fed Chairman Alan Greenspan decided to deal with the Tech Crash by *intentionally* creating another bubble… this time in <u>housing</u>.

This represented a move up the asset class pyramid. It also marked the beginning of what I call **The Era of Serial Bubbles**: the era in which the Fed dealt with each financial bubble and its subsequent collapse by intentionally creating *another bubble* in a more senior asset class.

Moving up the Asset Class Pyramid: Housing > Stocks

The financial media likes to talk about stocks as though everyone on the planet owns them. It's true that roughly half of American households have exposure to the stock market, but, almost all of this exposure is based on indirect purchases via 401(k)s and other stock-based retirement accounts.

Rarely, if ever, do individual Americans open brokerage accounts and start buying stocks directly. Indeed, even at the height of the Tech Bubble, the largest stock market bubble in US history driven by loose money from the Fed *and* a technology revolution, **only 21% of American households directly traded stocks.**

While stocks are not commonly owned, they are relatively easy and cheap to trade. You can buy a share in most publicly traded

88

companies for less than $100 and many for less than $20. And, you can do this in less than five minutes using an online trading account.

In this context, the Tech Bubble consisted of a relatively small percentage of Americans speculating in a highly liquid asset class. As such, the Tech Crash, while very painful for some, was not truly an "end of the world" event.

The Housing Bubble, by contrast, was a totally different situation.

Housing, as an asset class, is much more pervasively owned than stocks. Historically, between 50% and 60% of Americans have owned homes. And these were direct purchases made by Americans themselves, not indirect purchases via retirement accounts.

Moreover, houses are highly illiquid, expensive assets. Buying or selling a house, even under rapid circumstances, can take days if not weeks. And even a dilapidated house will cost $10,000 or more.

Indeed, for most Americans, buying a home represents the single largest financial transaction of their lives.

So, when the Greenspan/ Bernanke Fed opted to deal with the Tech Crash by creating a bubble in housing, it was choosing to deal with a collapse in a relatively minor, systemically insignificant asset class (tech stocks) by creating another bubble in a larger, much more systemically important asset class (housing).

The reason they did this was because they already knew the financial system was insolvent courtesy of the enormous debt bubble we've outlined (which I call the US's "Debt Mountain.") And, rather than let the Tech Crash be the needle that popped that underlying debt bubble, Greenspan/Bernanke decided it'd be better to create another bubble.

Here's how they did it.

Greenspan Makes Money "FREE"

As you'll recall from the last chapter, the Fed uses the Fed's Target Federal Funds Rate to control the "cost" of money in the financial system.

Historically, the Fed's Target Federal Funds rate has been closely aligned with economic growth. Chart 26 shows the Effective Federal Funds rate and US Gross Domestic Product growth going back to 1955. As you can see, the two are usually very closely aligned with the caveat that anytime the Fed hikes rates aggressively as it did in the late '70s, the economy usually rolls over.

Chart 26. Effective Federal Funds Rate and Year-Over -Year US Gross Domestic Product Growth Rate (1955-2000).

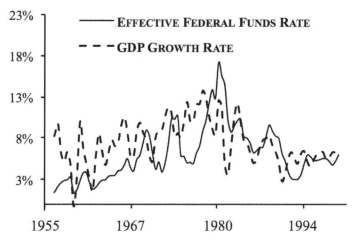

Note: Data adapted from Federal Reserve Bank of St. Louis (2017)[11,3]

There is a reason why the Effective Federal Funds Rate is usually kept close to the rate of growth for the US economy (except for when the Fed, while lead by those who actually wanted to maintain stability, intentionally "pumped the brakes" because it feared the economy and financial system were overheating).

Think of US economic growth as a rising tide that generally raises all ships (risk assets). If the economy is growing at 5%, just about every asset class that is linked to economic growth *should* be growing at a comparable rate, if not faster.

So if the Fed keeps interest rates too low (say 2%) while economic growth is at 5%, the Fed is basically handing out "free money" since you can borrow at 2% and invest the money in just about anything and pocket a 3% difference.

Historically, any time rates remained far below the pace of economic growth for long, it ALWAYS led to disaster. A great example concerns the 1970s when there were not one but two periods in which the Fed kept rates (the dotted line) too far below economic growth (the solid line) for too long (Chart 27).

Chart 27. Effective Federal Funds Rate and Year-Over-Year US Gross Domestic Product Growth Rate (1970-1981).

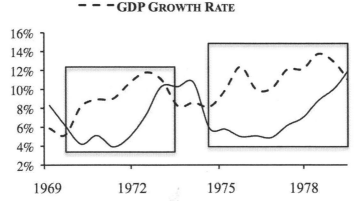

Note: Data adapted from Federal Reserve Bank of St. Louis (2017)[11,3]

As you may remember from Chapter 2, this decision, combined with Richard Nixon completely severing the US dollar from any link to gold, unleashed a bout of accelerated inflation during which prices for numerous goods rose **across the board by as much as 15% in the span of a few years.**

Put simply, the Fed's job is to keep rates relatively close to the pace of economic growth. Failing to do so, particularly for prolonged periods, always leads to disaster down the road.

With that in mind, consider what Alan Greenspan did in the aftermath of the Tech Crash.

The Tech Bubble peaked in early 2000 and began crashing soon after. Over the next two years, the NASDAQ would lose 75% of its value. To make matters worse, the US economy rolled over and entered a recession in 2001.

In response to this, the Greenspan Fed began cutting interest rates, making the cost of money "cheaper" for the financial system. I want to note that the pace of the rate cuts was *aggressive.* When Greenspan began cutting rates in December 2000, the Target Fed Funds rate was 6.4%. Within 12 months it was 1.82%.

Put another way, based on Greenspan's rate cuts, money became **nearly 72% *"cheaper" in the span of one year.***

This, by itself, suggests extreme panic on the part of the Fed. Remember, less than 25% of Americans owned stocks directly. And, the recession that began in 2000 was relatively shallow.

So why was the Fed panicking?

Because the Fed was terrified of the stock market's deflation spreading to the debt markets. At this point, the US Debt Mountain was so massive that even a whiff of debt deflation was systemically dangerous.

Put simply, the Fed's response to the Tech Crash was extreme. But it was what the Greenspan Fed did once the economy bottomed and began to recover that represented a truly tectonic shift for the Fed.

It was at this point, in the aftermath of the Tech Crash, that the Fed crossed the Financial Rubicon into the realm of intentionally creating asset bubbles.

Let me explain…

Under any normal circumstances, as soon as the US economy begins to bottom, the Fed begins raising interest rates to keep them in line with economic activity.

Not this time.

According to the Fed's own data, the US recession triggered by the Tech Crash ended around November 2001. But, Greenspan wasn't done flooding the system with "free money." Not by a long shot.

The Greenspan Fed actually cut rates in December 2001, bringing them to 1.75%. It then maintained this level for most of 2002 before cutting rates again to 1.25%. Still not finished, the Greenspan-led Fed cut rates even further to 1% in mid-2003, where they remained from July 2003 to July 2004.

Bear in mind, the recession had ended in **November 2001**, nearly a full THREE YEARS BEFORE. And by 2003, the economy hadn't just bottomed, it was ROARING at an annual GDP growth rate of 5%. And the Fed still had rates at just 1%!!!

Have a look at the Chart 28. Look at the massive gap between the Effective Federal Funds Rate and US Gross Domestic Product growth. And bear in mind, we're talking about a period of two to three years.

Chart 28. Effective Federal Funds Rate and Year-Over-Year US Gross Domestic Product Growth Rate (1999-2005).

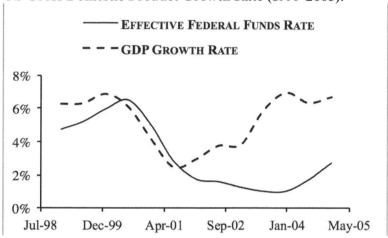

Note: Data adapted from Federal Reserve Bank of St. Louis (2017)[11, 3]

With the economy growing at 5%, maintaining interest rates at 1% was the equivalent of "giving" money away: you could borrow at 1%, invest in nearly anything tied to the economy, and see a 4% return annually with minimal risk.

That money had to go somewhere, and thanks to Congress, it went into housing where it rapidly became a systemic issue.

I'm talking about the Housing and Community Development Act of 1992 (which dramatically increased the number of people who qualified to buy a home).

The following is a technical breakdown of this bill and its impact on the mortgage market, which drives housing prices. If you're not interested in these details, feel free to skip ahead to the section titled *How the Housing Bubble Became a Global Systemic Risk.*

How the Housing Bubble Was Created

In the early to mid-'90s, US Congress launched a concentrated effort to make housing more affordable to more Americans.

To that end, in 1992, Congress passed the Housing and Community Development Act. What this bill did, was *require* certain massive players in the secondary mortgage market to spend at least 30% of their budget buying low quality mortgage loans.

Here's how it worked.

One of the provisions of Franklin Delano Roosevelt's New Deal back in 1938 was the creation of massive Government Sponsored Enterprises or privately held corporations that were *backed* by the US government.

These entities were supposed to allow the US government to direct capital in ways that the private market might not normally allow. They were, in a sense, a backstop for the financial system to insure that during crises, there were entities still willing to finance mortgages and the like.

The two best-known Government Sponsored Enterprises are the Federal National Mortgage Association, or Fannie Mae (Fannie for short), and the Federal Home Loan Mortgage Corporation, or Freddie Mac (Freddie for short).

Fannie and Freddie were meant to act as agents in the secondary mortgage market. What this means is that when a local bank or credit union makes a mortgage loan, instead of sitting on the loan, the bank or credit union could turn around and *sell* it to Fannie or Freddie on the secondary mortgage market.

This way, the bank didn't have to sit on the mortgage loan for 30 years but could use the cash generated from selling the mortgage to Fannie or Freddie to make *another loan*.

This system works just fine provided the banks are making mortgage loans to people who are able to afford them. Unfortunately, the Housing and Community Development Act of 1992 changed this.

In simple terms, what this law did was require Fannie and Freddie to spend 30% of their budget **buying mortgages that were made to those who were at or below the median income in their respective communities.**

What is a median?

A median is the perfect middle of anything. In terms of income, split any neighborhood in half by income and according to this legislation, Fannie and Freddie were required to spend 30% of their budgets buying mortgages that were made to **people who were in the bottom half.**

This was effectively a giant incentive for local banks to start lending money to people in lower income brackets. After all, if Fannie and Freddie were looking to spend $1 out of every $3 in their budgets buying low income mortgage loans from banks, you better believe that the banks are going to start making more loans to people in those income brackets.

However, there was one small problem.

Banks cannot make housing prices any cheaper. So if banks were to generate more mortgages to low income individuals, there was only one way to do it: by **lowering lending requirements.**

Historically, banks would avoid granting mortgages to people who had a high probability of not paying the bank back. After all, as long as the bank was responsible for the mortgage, the bank was at risk of losing money.

However, now that Fannie and Freddie were willing to buy these mortgages from banks on the secondary market, banks could lend money to anyone regardless of the risk and then flip the mortgage over to Fannie and Freddie for 100 cents on the dollar.

In the 30 years leading up to The Housing and Community Development Act of 1992, roughly 64% of Americans owned their homes.

<u>Between 1994 and 2000, homeownership in the United States rose from 64.2% to 67.5%.</u>

What this translated to was an additional 8.33 MILLION people becoming "homeowners." And most of them were individuals who couldn't truly afford to do so.

But wait, it gets worse.

Remember how I wrote earlier that the Federal Reserve *intentionally* created a housing bubble to combat the fallout from the Tech Crash?

The Federal Government was in on this as well.

As the Tech Crash unfolded in 2000, the government increased Fannie and Freddie's **<u>low-income mortgage quotas to 50%.</u>** Put another way, $1 out of every $2 Fannie and Freddie spent buying mortgages was required to be spent on **<u>high-risk/ low quality mortgages</u>**.

This, in turn, gave banks and mortgage lenders even *greater* financial incentives to lend to low-income borrowers, which meant *even lower* lending standards (sometimes lending to individuals with low credit scores, without any verification of income or assets/net worth).

Put simply, the US government opened the door to a housing bubble. And the Greenspan Fed financed it with "free" money.

You can see this in the Chart 29 below. Note that once the housing bill passed in 1992, the number of new single-family homes sold per year (the solid line) broke out of a multi-decade range and began to rise sharply. And, once Alan Greenspan made money "free" in 2000, housing prices (the dashed line) began to rise rapidly as well.

Chart 29: New US Single Family Homes Sold Per Year and Average US Home Price (1975-2008).

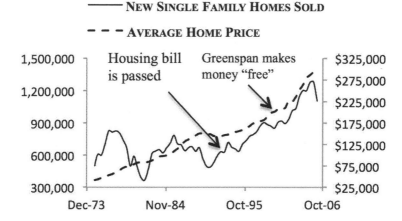

Note: Data adapted from Federal Reserve Bank of St. Louis (2017)[12]

Now, a housing bubble is <u>always</u> going to be a BIG issue due to both the political and financial significance of real estate as an asset class (when a housing bubble bursts, people lose their homes and the banks that made the mortgage loans go bust).

However, thanks to the rise of a special class of financial products on Wall Street, the housing bubble spread beyond the United States' borders and became a globally systemic issue.

How the US Housing Bubble Became a Global Systemic Risk

If you want to know why the US housing bubble of the mid-'00s was such a huge deal… as well as why all of the bailouts made during the 2008 crisis went to a select group of large banks, you first need to understand the derivatives markets.

What is a derivative?

Investopedia offers the following definition:

> *A derivative is a contract between two or more parties whose value is based on an agreed-upon underlying financial asset, index or security. Common underlying instruments include: bonds, commodities, currencies, interest rates, market indexes and stocks.*
>
> *Futures contracts, forward contracts, options, swaps and warrants are common derivatives. A futures contract, for example, is a derivative because its value is affected by the performance of the underlying contract. Similarly, a stock option is a derivative because its value is "derived" from that of the underlying stock.*
>
> Folger, Jean "What is a Derivative?"
> *Investopedia,* 4 April 2017, www.investopedia.com/ask/answers/12/derivative.asp

In simple terms, a derivative is essentially a bet between two parties about the future price or value of a particular asset.

Originally, derivatives were used as a means of hedging future price risk by individuals or companies who produced goods that experience significant price volatility (think oil, cattle, etc.).

For instance, if a cattle farmer was concerned about the future price he'd get for a herd of cattle when it comes time to slaughter them, he could *hedge* his risk by buying a derivative that gave him the right to sell his cattle at a particular price, no matter what the market turns out to be paying for cattle at slaughter time.

Put simply, derivatives were designed to minimize risk. And there are two types:

1) Regulated derivatives: derivatives that pass through open exchanges allowing for transparency and clear price discovery based on active market buying and selling.

2) Unregulated, Over the Counter derivatives: derivatives that are privately traded between "dealer" banks and are priced based on the dealers' internal valuation models or whatever they can get away with.

Guess which type of derivative is more popular with Wall Street?

Historically, the regulated derivatives market was larger than the Over the Counter one. However, as the US Debt Mountain grew, banks began moving aggressively into the Over the Counter derivatives market space, with a particular focus on derivatives related to interest rates (bond yields).

By the time the mid-'90s rolled around, the Over the Counter derivatives market had surpassed both the regulated derivatives market… and the United States' Gross Domestic Product!

The first data available to the public pegs the notional value of the Over the Counter derivatives market at $16.8 trillion in the fourth quarter of 1995. By way of comparison, the United States' annual economic output was around $7.8 trillion at the time.

Put another way, as early as 1995, the notional value of the Over the Counter derivatives market was already over 200% of US Gross Domestic Product.

Now, Wall Street would argue that not *all* of these derivatives trades represented "money at risk." Remember, these types of derivatives are basically bets on the *value* of underlying assets.

So the value of the bets is not the same as the value of the underlying assets.

I realize this is getting confusing, so let me give you a hypothetical example.

Let's say your car is worth $10,000 today. You and I bet each other $1,000 that in five years' time, the car will either be worth more (you win) or worth less (I win) than its current value.

This is a binary bet (meaning there are only two potential outcomes) with a value of $1,000. And bear in mind, the value of the car is $10,000, while the value of our bet is just $1,000.

Still with me? Good, because unregulated Over the Counter derivatives are more complicated than this.

Now, let's imagine that our bet is based on a very specific outcome. Imagine that we are betting on whether or not your car will be worth *exactly* $12,000 in five years' time. And imagine that the initial value of this bet is $1,000, but that the value of the bet fluctuates based on the value of the car at any given time.

For instance, let's say that the bet is worth $1,000 when the car is trading at a value of $10,000 today. But let's say that a year from now, a car magazine is published in which experts claim that this particular make and model of car is now worth only $9,000.

Is the value of our bet now worth more or less?

It's now worth *less* because the car now has to appreciate *$3,000* in value over *four years* as opposed to appreciating $2,000 in five years as per our initial bet.

Put another way, if the car has gone from $10,000 in value to $9,000 in one year, the odds of it being worth $12,000 at the time of our bet expiring are much smaller. After all, the value of the car is moving in the wrong direction.

Now let's add a final component. Imagine that we can SELL our bet to other people who might want to speculate on the car's value. And imagine that there is no objective guide for measuring the car's value and that you and I are permitted to decide the car's value ourselves.

That's **the equivalent of the Over the Counter derivative market. And in 1994 there were nearly $17 trillion worth of these bets floating around the US financial system.**

This created a systemic issue for the big banks that traded these derivatives because roughly 64% of Over the Counter derivatives were related to interest rates. We'll delve into this issue more in our next chapter, but for now, the point is that if a significant debt collapse hit, interest rates would spike (bond yields rise when bond prices fall) and nearly $11 trillion in Over the Counter derivatives contracts would have to adjust in value.

This would literally implode Wall Street and the financial markets.

Lest you think I am getting into conspiracy theory here, consider the following verified story.

In 1998, soon to be chairperson of the Commodity Futures Trading Commission (a derivatives exchange for *regulated* derivatives), Brooksley Born, approached Alan Greenspan, Bob Rubin, and Larry Summers (the three heads of economic policy for the United States at the time) about the Over the Counter derivatives market.

Born said she thought Over the Counter derivatives should be reined in and regulated because the market was getting too big to contain if a crisis hit. The response from Greenspan and the others was that if she pushed for regulation of Over the Counter derivatives the markets would **"implode."**

<u>So Greenspan knew the Over the Counter derivatives issue was a systemic issue as far back as 1998.</u>

This again, helps to explain why Greenspan chose to address the Tech Crash by creating a Housing Bubble. It also helps to explain why Over the Counter derivatives became an even bigger problem in the build up to the crisis of 2008.

By turning a blind eye to Wall Street's Over the Counter derivatives bonanza and refusing to let bad debts clear through the system via the Tech Crash, Greenspan was setting the stage for an even bigger crash.

After all, he was now actively creating a bubble in an even more senior asset class (housing) that was owned by an even greater percentage of Americans (69% vs. 21% for stocks), and permitting Wall Street to engage in even more reckless Over the Counter derivatives trades.

Chart 30 is what the US financial system looked like during the Tech Crash when you include Over the Counter derivatives.

Chart 30: Total US Debt Securities, US Gross Domestic Product, and Notional Value of Derivatives Outstanding at US Commercial Banks, Trillions US Dollars (1946-2000).

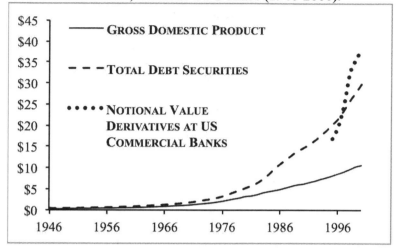

Note: Data adapted from Federal Reserve Bank of St. Louis and Office of the Comptroller of the Currency (2017)[3, 13]

Chart 31 is what it looked like by the time 2008 rolled around.

Chart 31: Total US Debt Securities, US Gross Domestic Product, and Notional Value of Derivatives Outstanding at US Commercial Banks, Trillions US Dollars (1946-2008).

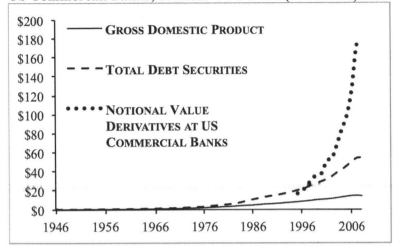

Note: Data adapted from Federal Reserve Bank of St. Louis and Office of the Comptroller of the Currency (2017)[3, 13]

If you want a simple way of reading the above chart consider that the solid line represents the actual economy. The dashed line represents total debt in the financial system. The dotted line represents Wall Street placing unregulated bets on where the value of both would be in the future, particularly regarding housing prices.

Put another way, with a larger, even more systemically important asset class (real estate) now in a bubble and the ability to trade an unlimited number of derivatives based on this asset class, **Wall Street went completely bonkers selling these products to financial institutions around the globe.**

By the time the housing bubble burst in 2008, the United States' mortgage market was $14 trillion in size. But, thanks to Over the Counter derivatives, the actual risk related to the US housing market was well north of $175 trillion in size. That was more than TEN TIMES the size of US Gross Domestic Product at the time.

And this whole mess can be justly laid at Alan Greenspan's feet. As Chairman of the Federal Reserve in the build up to this, Greenspan was responsible for regulating the banks.

Remember my campus cop metaphor from last chapter? The one about Greenspan serving as a campus cop whose job it was to show up and shut down parties (excessive risk taking) once they start to get out of control?

Well instead of doing that, Greenspan did the equivalent of showing up at the party, giving the kids the city's AMEX card and telling them, *"have as much fun as you want! I'm taking the rest of the night off!"*

This was the true Greenspan legacy: that of allowing the financial system to become one gigantic unregulated bet, fueled by cheap debt and "free money."

In 2008, the whole mess came crashing down. Housing prices peaked in 2006, leading to debt deflation hitting the mortgage-backed securities markets (a segment of the Over the Counter derivatives market).

As these securities began to deflate in value, the issue quickly became systemic in nature as every financial institution with exposure to the Over the Counter derivatives market was no longer certain of the value of its holdings.

This culminated in the panic sell off of the 2008 Crash: a time when the stock market lost over a third of its value in a single year.

However, by 2008 Greenspan was long gone, cashing in on a high paying gig at a major **bond** investment firm. Ben Bernanke, the supposed deflation expert, was at the helm of the Fed and facing the very situation he claimed would never hit the United States…

Debt deflation, or "it" as he called debt deflation in his famous speech.

For the first time since ending the Gold Standard in 1933, the US financial system was facing a genuine debt collapse.

Like his predecessor, Alan Greenspan back in 2001, in 2008 Ben Bernanke had a choice. That choice was, *"do I go down in history as the guy who let the system implode, kicking off another Great Depression… or do I reflate the system with another bubble and pass this mess off to the next person?"*

Bernanke, like Greenspan, chose the second option. However, by this point the US Debt Mountain was so massive that he would have to engage in even more extreme monetary policy.

So Bernanke took the very problems that nearly blew up Wall Street (garbage debt, toxic derivatives, and excessive risk taking) and allowed them to spread onto the US Government's public balance sheet.

Put simply, Bernanke created a bubble in US sovereign bonds (or Treasuries).

And, because US Treasuries were now the bedrock of the US financial system (having replaced the US dollar which had replaced gold), this became The Everything Bubble: a bubble in every asset class under the sun.

Good. God. Almighty.

CHAPTER 5:
THE EVERYTHING BUBBLE

To recap the last chapter…

From 1987 until 2006 when he stepped down as Fed Chair, Alan Greenspan turned a blind eye to obvious risks percolating in the US financial system. His mistakes were numerous, but the biggest one by far was to allow the US Debt Mountain to grow exponentially without doing anything to stop it.

The end result was that by the time the Tech Bubble burst in 2000, the US Debt Mountain had reached such heights that even a "whiff" of debt deflation could cause a systemic crisis.

As a result of this, Greenspan, under the influence of his advisor, "deflation expert" Ben Bernanke, opted to deal with the Tech Bubble by *intentionally* creating a new bubble in housing.

This represented a move up the asset class food chain. Housing was a larger, more systemically important asset class than stocks.

And, because Greenspan and his economic cohorts *also* chose to turn a blind eye to Wall Street's Over the Counter derivatives schemes, the housing bubble went from a $14 trillion crisis in US real estate to a $100+ trillion bank solvency issue, infecting the entire global financial system.

Greenspan left the Fed in 2006 (ironically right around the time housing prices peaked), at which time Bernanke was promoted to Fed Chairman.

What followed was the housing bubble burst, triggering the single worst financial crisis in 80+ years, as tens of trillions of dollars' worth of derivatives bets proved worth less than the big banks had previously claimed.

In the simplest of terms, the dreaded debt deflation that Bernanke claimed was preventable, had finally hit. It started in mortgage loans, then spread to mortgage-backed securities, consumer loans, commercial paper loans and finally stock prices.

I've shown the below chart before, but, my intention here is to stress that this marked the first period of real debt deflation in the United States in 80+ years...**and it was just a tiny blip in a mountain of debt (see Chart 32)!**

Chart 32: Debt Deflation of the 2008 Crisis For Total US Debt Securities and Its Impact on US Gross Domestic Product, Trillions US Dollars (1945-2016)

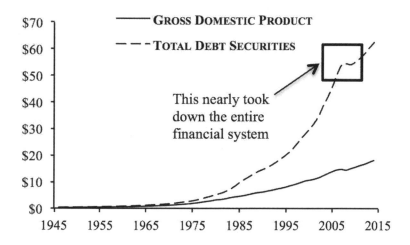

Note: Data adapted from Federal Reserve Bank of St. Louis (2017)[3]

Ben Bernanke, like Alan Greenspan before him, decided to deal with this systemic issue by creating *another* bubble in an even more senior asset class... US sovereign bonds or Treasuries.

This marked the beginning of the end game for the Fed's monetary policy in our current financial system.

As I've explained throughout the first half of this book, US Treasuries are the **standard for measuring all risk in the global financial system.** In particular, the yield on the 10-Year US Treasury is considered the "risk free" rate of return: the rate against which all other risk assets are compared and priced.

Stocks, commodities, oil, mortgage rates, home prices, literally *everything,* is valued based on its risk level relative to this yield. So, if this yield is pushed to abnormally low levels (creating a bubble in bonds forces bond prices up and yields down) then **all risk assets in the financial system would adjust accordingly.**

So, when Bernanke opted to create a bubble in US sovereign bonds, he was *literally* creating a bubble in EVERYTHING.

As shocking as this is, you have to appreciate the hubris. The various financial "villains" we've chronicled thus far (Franklin Delano Roosevelt, Richard Nixon, Alan Greenspan) had all fantasized about bending the financial system to their personal agendas in one way of another.

However, NONE of them had outright attempted to dominate the entire global financial system like Ben Bernanke. He literally believed he could halt deflation by cornering the bond market, thereby controlling ***all financial risk in the world.***

To do this, the Bernanke Fed pushed for three major policies:

1) The abandonment of "mark to market" accounting standards (this would halt the deflationary collapse of the derivatives markets and permit banks to value their assets at absurd valuations, thereby reflating the US Debt Mountain).

2) Cutting the Fed's Target Federal Funds Rate to zero in order to make US bond payments as small as possible (thereby allowing the United States to go on a debt binge far in excess of anything before).

3) Attempting to corner the US sovereign bond market via various Quantitative Easing, or QE programs (monetary programs through which the Fed printed new money to buy US sovereign bonds and other assets, thereby establishing a "dumb money" investor who would backstop the bond market).

If any of the above terms seem confusing, don't worry; we'll be tackling all of these concepts in the pages ahead.

However, in order to understand how the Bernanke Fed accomplished #1, you first need to understand how banks are required to value assets on their balance sheets.

The following is a technical breakdown of bank accounting standards in the United States. If you're not interested in these details, feel free to skip ahead to the section titled ***Bernanke Buys Garbage and Pushes To Have It Rated Gold.***

Mark to Market Vs. Mark to Model (or Make Believe)

When it comes to buying or selling assets (read: anything), there are two types (or classes) of assets in the world: liquid and non-liquid.

This is not a reference to the physical state of the asset (we're not talking about whether it is something you can pour or not), but how easy it is to buy or sell the asset in the economy.

Liquid assets are assets that are easy to buy or sell. The term stems from the notion that these assets "flow" through the economy easily.

Most of the transactions in which you engage during your lifetime will involve liquid assets. Buying gasoline for your car, buying groceries at the store, even buying a new pair of shoes…

these are all transactions involving liquid assets.

Illiquid assets, on the other hand, are items that are *not* easy to buy or sell. Your house is a great example of this: buying or selling a house takes days, if not weeks or even months to accomplish.

When it comes to liquidity, size usually matters, meaning the greater an asset's price, the less liquid it tends to be (buying a candy bar is a lot easier than buying a house or a 50-story skyscraper).

Now, for any transaction, regardless of the liquidity status of the assets involved, a key issue is determining the "value" of what's being bought or sold.

For most items in the economy (candy bars, automobiles, etc.) the value is simply the "price" at which the item is being sold. If you buy a candy bar for $1.50, then it's valued at $1.50 (until you eat it, of course).

This is called "mark to market" accounting, meaning the item's value is effectively what someone in the economy (also called "the market") would be willing to pay for it at any given time.

It's important to note that even illiquid assets usually use "mark to market" accounting. A great example is your home: even though this is an illiquid asset, its value is usually relatively easy to determine based on the sales prices of other comparable homes in the area.

As a result, pretty much every transaction the average person engages in during his or her life will feature "mark to market" accounting, regardless of whether or not the asset involved is liquid.

This used to be the case for banks... at least until they started messing around with "Over the Counter" derivatives.

As you'll recall from the last chapter, Over the Counter derivatives are unregulated financial securities that banks either trade with one another or sell to large entities such as state governments or multinational corporations.

I mentioned before that large banks prefer trading/peddling Over the Counter derivatives as opposed to regular, regulated derivatives. There's a reason for this: because Over the Counter derivatives are unregulated, they are much more difficult to price.

For one thing, the fact that no such securities ever existed before means a lack of historical transaction data. And, because these securities are not forced to pass through an exchange where they would be valued by the market, the banks get to value these derivatives using a different type of accounting standard called "mark to model" accounting.

Mark to model accounting means an asset is being valued based on a "model," in this case, the bank's own internal "model" of risk and value.

Put another way, provided the banks can come up with some kind of justification for value, they can price these derivatives at virtually any price they like. For this reason, when you see the phrase "market to model" it's pretty safe to assume it really means, "make believe."

After all, asking a bank to accurately value an illiquid asset that it is selling (and that no one else can accurately price) is like asking a raging alcoholic to determine his blood alcohol level using his own judgment instead of a Breathalyzer.

However, because entities ranging from corporations to county governments were keen to use Wall Street's Over the Counter derivatives to hide their debt liabilities or boost their earnings, and because the banks selling these instruments were still held in high esteem prior to 2008, everyone played along with this scheme.

As the Over the Counter derivatives markets grew throughout the 1970s until the mid-2000s, so did the complexity of these securities, as well as the complexity of the internal models banks were using to justify the "value" of these assets.

By the time housing prices peaked in 2006, Wall Street had managed to package absolute garbage securities (Over the Counter derivatives comprised of thousands of mortgages that were loaned out to people who could never pay them back) as if they were made of solid gold.

Remember this chart (Chart #33)?

Chart 33: Total US Debt Securities, US Gross Domestic Product, and Notional Value of Derivatives Outstanding at US Commercial Banks, Trillions US Dollars (1946-2008).

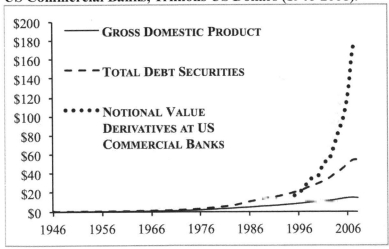

Note: Data adapted from Federal Reserve Bank of St. Louis and Office of the Comptroller of the Currency (2017)[3, 13]

Consider the solid line to be economic activities that are "mark to market," the dashed line concerns economic activities that are "marked kind of to market," and the dotted line represents financial (not economic) activities that are "mark to model."

Bear in mind that Chart 33 only concerns US-based banks. Globally, by the time the 2008 Crisis hit, the notional value of the Over the Counter derivatives market was in the ballpark of $1 QUADRILLION (1,000 trillions).

In this context, the 2008 meltdown was first triggered by large institutional investors realizing that tens if not hundreds of trillions of dollars' worth of Over the Counter derivatives related to US mortgages were not, in fact, worth anything close what Wall Street's "mark to model" accounting standards claimed when the banks had sold them.

Remember, Wall Street had been selling these securities to *everyone* (governments, corporations, hedge funds, pension funds, other banks etc.). So, the idea that these "assets" were mispriced and actually worth much less (or potentially even worthless) meant a systemic exposure to deflation in the derivatives markets.

Enter Ben Bernanke.

To stop the derivatives market from imploding and taking down the financial system, Bernanke had to reinstill investor confidence in the Over the Counter derivatives market and its methods for valuing these securities.

The problem was that in the depths of the 2008 crisis, NO ONE wanted to own this garbage, let alone buy it as an investment.

So Bernanke had the Federal Reserve print money and then use this money to buy these assets via a process called Quantitative Easing, or QE. And he didn't just buy a few Over the Counter derivatives… he bought $1.35 TRILLION worth of them.

Worst of all, because he was doing this via the Federal Reserve, technically he was using the public's checkbook to do it.

Bernanke Buys Garbage and Pushes To Have It Rated Gold

Quantitative Easing, or QE, sounds like something complicated and technical, but in reality it's simply the process through which a central bank prints money and uses it to buy assets.

On November 26, 2008, when the Fed announced its first QE program, Fed leadershp was explicit as to the purpose: to give the Government Sponsored Entities (Fannie and Freddie) a means to unload their garbage mortgage-backed securities.

And not just a few of these securities, $600 billion worth!

When that didn't prove to be enough to convince everyone that the Fed was willing to backstop the Over the Counter derivatives market, Bernanke had this program expanded by another $750 billion, bringing the total amount of mortgage-backed securities the Fed would buy to $1.35 TRILLION (roughly the size of Spain's economy).

This solved one problem: the firms sitting on hundreds of billions of dollars' worth of garbage mortgage-backed securities now had a buyer (the Fed) to whom they could sell this stuff.

However, this didn't stop the crisis of confidence that permeated the financial system. After all, the notional value of the Over the Counter derivatives market was still well above $700 trillion. So the Fed couldn't possibly buy all of it.

With that in mind, starting in late 2008, the Bernanke Fed and other financial regulators lobbied hard for the Financial Accounting Standards Board (the regulator in charge of accounting standards for the banks) to suspend mark to market accounting standards for the big banks regarding their mortgage-backed securities and other Over the Counter derivatives.

Yes, Bernanke wanted it to be official policy that banks could value their assets using mark to model accounting standards, or "make believe."

Again, you have to admire the man's hubris.

Up until this point, when banks went to value a mortgage-backed security, they were forced to do so using the latest sales price at which a similar asset had been sold. Before the 2008 crisis, this wasn't a big deal because the banks had been selling other, similar derivatives at ridiculously high "make believe" valuations.

However, during the 2008 crisis, many firms were selling these securities at fire sale prices. As a result of this, those banks and firms that continued to own Over the Counter derivatives were forced to revalue their own securities at similar prices levels.

This was quickly leading to many banks facing solvency issues as their derivatives portfolios were being repriced lower and lower.

This all changed on April 3, 2009, when the Financial Accounting Standards Board suspended mark to market accounting standards on any assets that banks found to be illiquid or difficult to sell (not just Over the Counter derivatives).

This policy change, the result of pressure from the Bernanke Fed, gave the banks the ability to value their assets at whatever level they wanted. Indeed, according to the new rules, banks could even tell their clients, *"the market value for this asset is wrong, the TRUE value is what we say it is."*

Put simply, the banks could now value their illiquid, Over the Counter derivatives at 100 cents on the dollar. Even better for the banks, the Fed was now willing to buy the worst of these securities from them at these "make believe" valuations via its QE programs.

The end result?

The derivatives market stopped imploding and began to reflate again (see Chart 34).

Chart 34: Notional Value of Derivatives Outstanding at US Commercial Banks, Trillions US Dollars (2000-2012).

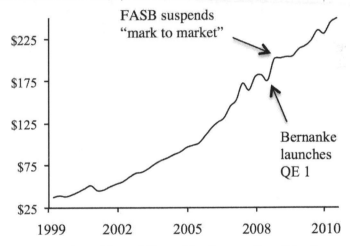

Note: Data adapted from Office of the Comptroller of the Currency (2017)[13]

But, Bernanke wasn't done yet. Not by a long shot.

Yes, he'd stop a deflationary implosion in illiquid debt instruments like mortgage-backed securities... but he wanted more than this; he wanted to employ this same scheme with US sovereign bonds or Treasuries.

Put simply, Bernanke wanted to control ALL global financial risk. He wanted to create an Everything Bubble.

Here's how he did it.

Bernanke Makes Greenspan Look Like an Amateur

Recall from Chapter 4, *The Fed Crosses the Financial Rubicon,* that back in the early 2000s then-Fed Chair Alan Greenspan used the Fed's Target Federal Funds Rate (the cost of money in the financial system) to make money "free."

By way of review, Greenspan cut rates from a peak of 6.4% in late 2000 down to 1.00% in mid-2003. He then kept rates below the pace of economic growth for three years, essentially making money "free" (with the cost of money 3%-4% below the rate of economic growth you could borrow money and invest it just about anywhere in the economy and pocket the difference for an easy profit).

Doing this funded the housing bubble.

To create a bubble in US sovereign bonds, Bernanke took Greenspan's policy to an even greater extreme.

Greenspan cut the Fed's Target Federal Funds Rate down to 1.00%. He then kept it well below the pace of US economic growth for three years.

Bernanke cut the Fed's Target Federal Funds Rate down to 0.25% or effectively ZERO. He then kept it below the pace of US economic growth for SEVEN years.

This was the famous Zero Interest Rate Policy or ZIRP.

Prior to Ben Bernanke, the Fed had NEVER implemented ZIRP before. Even during the Great Depression when the economy was barely moving, or during World War II when the US was issuing debt at a staggering pace to fund its war efforts, the Fed's Effective Federal Funds rate was 4% and 2.00%, respectively.

Put simply, Ben Bernanke took interest rates to their **all time lows.** He didn't just make money free relative to economic growth, he made it free *literally* (with rates at 0.25% the interest payment on a $1 million loan was a mere **$2,500 per year)**.

And he did this for SEVEN years.

I realize this is getting a bit technical, so let's look at some images. Greenspan did this… (Chart 35).

Chart 35. Effective Federal Funds Rate and Year Over Year US Gross Domestic Product Growth Rate (1999-2006).

Note: Data adapted from Federal Reserve Bank of St. Louis (2017)[3,11]

This created the Housing Bubble: a 1-in-100 year bubble in housing prices.

Bernanke did this… (Chart 36).

Chart 36. Effective Federal Funds Rate and Year Over Year US Gross Domestic Product Growth Rate (2008-2014).

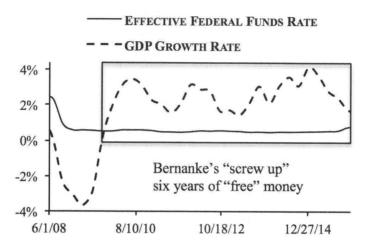

Note: Data adapted from Federal Reserve Bank of St. Louis (2017)[3,11]

The impact of this policy was to create a bubble in short-term US Treasuries.

Remember from Chapter 2, *The Building of a Debt Mountain,* Treasury yields represent the rate of interest the US government pays on its debt. In this regard, the lower US Treasury yields fall, the *cheaper* it is for the United States to issue debt.

Well, the yields on short-term Treasuries, (think 52 weeks or less), track the Fed's Target Federal Funds Rate. So when Bernanke cut the Fed's Target Federal Funds Rate effectively to zero, he was also pulling down the **borrowing cost for the United States government on its short-term debt obligations.**

Chart 37. Effective Federal Funds Rate and 3-Month US Treasury Bill Yield (2006-2012).

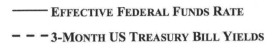

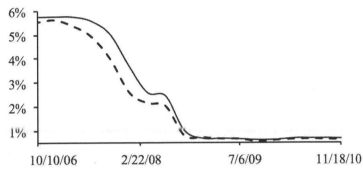

Note: Data adapted from Federal Reserve Bank of St. Louis (2017)[11, 14]

With short-term borrowing costs for the United States now at **all-time lows** thanks to Bernanke, the US government went on a massive spending spree, running $1+ trillion deficits for FOUR YEARS STRAIGHT.

This means the United States government was spending over $1 trillion in excess of the taxes it was collecting every single year from 2009 to 2013. And it's not as if things became fiscally sane in 2014: the United States government ran annual deficits of $400+ billion that year as well as in 2015 and 2016.

As a result of this, in the eight years following the 2008 crisis, the United States issued more debt than it had in ALL of its previous 230+ years **combined.** You can see the exact point at which the slope of the United States' public Debt Mountain began to go vertical in 2008. I've circled in in Chart 38.

Chart 38. US Public Debt, Trillions US Dollars (1966-2016).

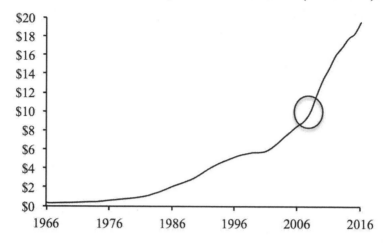

Note: Data adapted from Federal Reserve Bank of St. Louis (2017)[5]

It is also critical to note the *pace* at which this happened. Below is the US government's public debt as a percentage of its Gross Domestic Product running back to 1966 (see Chart 39).

Note that in 2008, the US Debt to GDP ratio was just 64%. Within just five years it had risen to 100%.

Chart 39. US Public Debt to Gross Domestic Product Ratio (1966-2016).

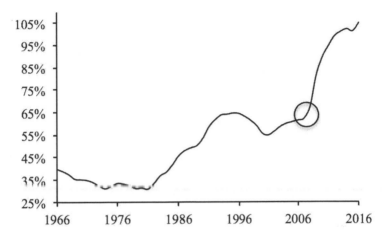

Note: Data adapted from Federal Reserve Bank of St. Louis (2017)[6]

This was Bernanke's Legacy: the Bond Bubble.

However, Uncle Sam wasn't the only one taking advantage of Bernanke's "free" money. By maintaining interest rates well below the pace of economic growth, Bernanke wasn't just pulling down short-term Treasury yields, **he was pulling down the entire risk landscape of the United States financial system.**

Consider corporate bonds.

Corporations, like the government, will issue debt if they are not generating enough money to finance an expense (or, if they're looking to fund a particular project without wiping out their cash flow).This debt is called a corporate bond.

Lending money to a company is riskier than lending to the US Government (remember, the latter can always print money to pay you back). Because of this, the yields on corporate bonds are generally higher than the yields on "risk-free" short-term Treasury Bills as investors demand a higher return to compensate for the greater risk.

However, corporate bonds generally track short-term Treasury Bills. So, if the yields on short-term Treasury Bills are trading at extraordinarily low levels because the Fed is keeping rates too low (as it did under Bernanke's watch post-2008), the yields on corporate bonds will eventually drop as well.

Chart 40 shows the yield on the 3-Month Treasury Bill (solid line), as well as the yields on 2-year high quality corporate bonds (dashed line) from 2008 onwards.

Note that it took a few years after the crisis was resolved, but eventually corporate bond yields began to trend lower toward the abnormally low T-bill yields.

Chart 40. 3-Month US Treasury Bill Yield and 2-Year High Quality Corporate Bond Yield (2006-2016).

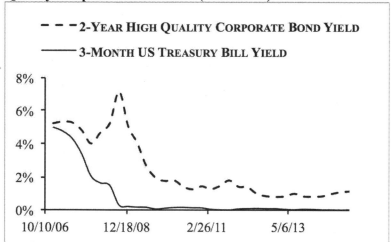

Note: Data adapted from Federal Reserve Bank of St. Louis (2017)[14, 15]

Here is literal proof that "risk" in the system was adjusting to abnormally low levels based on Bernanke keeping the "risk free" rate so low.

Corporations, noting that the market was effectively rating them at abnormally low risk levels, took advantage of this to start issuing debt at a record pace.

It took 50+ years for the US corporate debt market to reach $3 trillion in size. Thanks to Bernanke's ZIRP, it grew by roughly another $3 trillion (doubling) in just eight years. To put this into perspective, at this level US corporate debt was larger than the economy of Japan (see Chart 41).

Chart 41: Total US Corporate Debt, Trillions US Dollars (1951-2016).

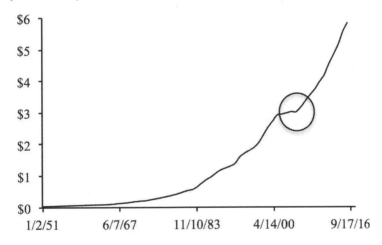

Note: Data adapted from Federal Reserve Bank of St. Louis (2017)[7]

As you'll recall from Chapter 2, *The Building of a Debt Mountain*, the United States issues Treasuries for numerous time periods ranging from four weeks to 30 years. And, while Bernanke's ZIRP primarily impacted short-term T-bills or US Government bonds with terms of 52 weeks or less, it did little to impact long-term Treasury bonds which remained at risk of potential debt deflation.

In order to fix this, the Bernanke Fed embarked on several large-scale programs through which it either printed money to buy longer-term Treasury bonds (Quantitative Easing 2 or QE 2 in 2010) or sold short-term Treasuries it already owned in order to buy long-term Treasuries (Operation Twist in 2011).

Here's how these programs worked.

Bernanke Provides the Ultimate "Dumb Money" Buyer For the Bond Markets

One of the most common adages in investing is the famous phrase, *"buy low and sell high."* What this means is that your goal should be to invest in something when it's cheap or trading at a "low" level… and, then sell it when it's expensive or trading at a "high" level for a profit.

What this phrase leaves out is that in order for something to move from "low" to "high," it will require a greater number of buyers (or more capital) to buy it, pushing it up.

This is the "greater fool" or "dumb money" part of investing: namely, that unless you are buying something specifically for its yield or payment, you are basically buying it in the hope that someone else will want to buy it from you later at a higher price.

Normally, when you're buying something this is just a hope. But thanks to Ben Bernanke's Fed policies, when it came to buying longer-term US Treasuries from 2010 onwards, **this hope was in fact a guarantee.**

In November 2010, the Bernanke Fed announced QE 2, a program through which the Fed would print $600 billion and use this new money to buy US Treasuries over the course of six months.

What this meant was that the Fed was literally broadcasting to the bond markets, *"hey everyone, for the next six months we're going to be buying Treasuries at various fixed intervals… oh and by the way, we won't be too picky about the price we pay."*

Put simply, Ben Bernanke provided the ultimate "dumb money" buyer to the bond markets: a buyer who literally broadcast in advance when he would be buying and made it clear that price was not an issue.

Any bond trader with a functioning brain heard this announcement and began piling into US Treasuries. After all, if you KNOW someone else is willing to buy your bonds at a set point in the future, why not "front-run" them and buy the bonds yourself first, then turn around and sell to this buyer at a higher price for an easy profit?

This is precisely what happened as every bond manager/ bond trader under the sun bought Treasuries to front-run the Fed. As a result, yields on the 10-Year Treasury collapsed to new lows (see Chart 42).

Chart 42: 10-Year US Treasury Yield (2010-2012).

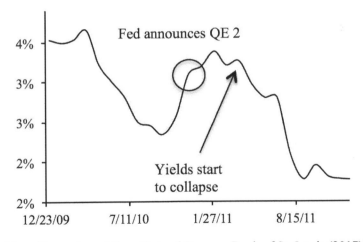

Note: Data adapted from Federal Reserve Bank of St. Louis (2017)[4]

To provide some perspective here, the last time the yield on the 10-Year Treasury was this low was during the build up to World War II, when capital was fleeing Europe for the United States. Put another way, Bernanke's monetary policies induced a capital flight to US sovereign bonds that has only been matched by a period in which the entire world was about to go to war.

QE 2 ended in June of 2011. And, this presented the Bernanke Fed with a problem. After all, it had essentially rigged the financial system by providing a "dumb money" buyer for Treasuries and other debt assets virtually non-stop for three years since December 2008, creating a bubble in the risk free rate of return for the entire financial system

That rig was now ending. And to make matters worse, yields were beginning to rise on the long-end of the Treasury curve (Treasuries with maturation periods of 20 or 30 years).

Bernanke couldn't simply have the Fed announce another massive QE program to buy long-bonds because QE had already become politically toxic (the Fed's QE 2 program had unleashed a wave of global inflation).

So, in 2011 the Bernanke Fed opted for a new asset purchase program called Operation Twist. Through it, the Fed would sell the short-term Treasuries it owned and use the money generated from these sales to buy long-term Treasuries.

However, by this point Bernanke had also come to discover the power of verbal intervention on the markets.

After three years of near non-stop Fed monetary intervention in the bond markets, bond prices were now hanging on Bernanke's every public statement. And he knew it. So instead of simply launching Operation Twist, he first teased the markets with the prospect of it for several months.

This would become a hallmark of Bernanke's tenure at the Fed: utilizing verbal intervention, or the promise of additional monetary stimulus, for months before unveiling an actual program. He found this strategy to be so effective at inducing investors to front-run the Fed (thereby pushing bonds yields even lower) that he would later write that *"monetary policy is 98 percent talk and only two percent action."*

Operation Twist began in September 2011. It was extended in June 2012 and finally came to completion in December 2012 (by which time Bernanke had already announced *another* QE program, QE 3, a $45 billion a month program to buy mortgage debt).

Throughout this period, the Fed sold off short-term Treasuries and bought long-term Treasuries. This provided a near perpetual "dumb money" buyer for long-bonds (the bonds most at risk of debt deflation should it return). The 30-Year Treasury yield dropped accordingly as investors once again front-ran the Fed's purchases (see Chart 43).

Chart 43: 30-Year US Treasury Yield (2010-2013).

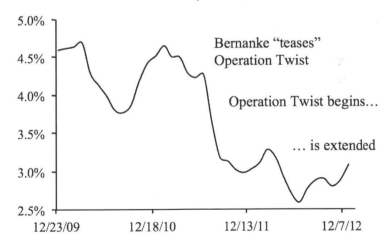

Note: Data adapted from Federal Reserve Bank of St. Louis (2017)[16]

I realize all of this is starting to get quite technical. So let me lay this out in very broad terms.

Starting in 2008, Ben Bernanke set about dealing with the housing crash by *intentionally* creating a bubble in bonds. This represented the single largest financial rig in history as Bernanke was creating a bubble in the risk-free rate of return for the entire financial system.

He did this by:

1) Cutting the Fed's Target Federal Funds rate to zero (making money "free") and keeping it there for seven years.

2) Creating the ultimate "dumb money" buyer for US sovereign bonds or Treasuries: a buyer who could print new money to buy bonds at any time and who had no interest in profiting from those purchases (an indiscriminant buyer).

The first policy provided a near endless supply of liquidity to financial institutions. The second gave them the easiest trade in the world: front-running the Fed's bond purchases by buying US Treasuries only to turn around and sell these bonds to the Fed at higher prices.

And so, the sovereign bond bubble was created. And because sovereign bonds were the bedrock of the fiat financial system, the risk-free rate against which all other risk is measured, **<u>EVERY-THING</u>** went into a bubble.

We've already assessed how this created a bubble in the debt markets (both sovereign and corporate), but what about other assets, like stocks for instance?

Glad you asked.

Low Treasury Yields = Buy Stocks

Remember, the yield on the 10-Year Treasury is the "risk free" rate of return, or the rate against which all risk in the US financial system is measured.

Stocks are part of the "risk" to which I am referring.

When you buy a stock, you are becoming an equity holder in the company. As such, you are making a much riskier investment than if you invested in a US Treasury or in the corporate bonds issued by the same company: unlike the US government, if the company goes broke it can't just print money to pay you back. Moreover, whatever money the company *does* have after bankruptcy will go to its bond holders long before equity holders, such as yourself, see a dime.

Because of this increased risk, stock investors require a greater "reward" in the form of greater potential gains from their investments. This is why stocks are considered a more "exciting" asset class: when they move, they move a lot more than bonds.

Put simply, stocks are riskier, but more exciting, than bonds.

However, even this "excitement" can be traced back to US Treasury yields and the "risk free" rate of return for the financial system. Indeed, the most common financial models used by investment firms and financial advisors recommend just how much money you should put into the stock market based on…wait for it… where US Treasury yields are trading.

The model I'm referring to is called The Fed Model (though the Fed has never formally endorsed it) and it is one of the most widely used models for asset allocation in finance.

Here's how it works.

The Fed model is based on the notion that the stock market's earnings yield (the ratio of stock profits to stock prices) should ultimately trade in-line with the yield on long-term US Treasuries (Treasuries issued for 10 years or more).

Put simply, stock profits divided by stock prices should equal Treasury yields. I realize this is difficult to visualize; so Chart 44 plots this relationship.

Chart 44: US Stock Market Earnings Yield and 10-Year US Treasury Yield (1982-2016).

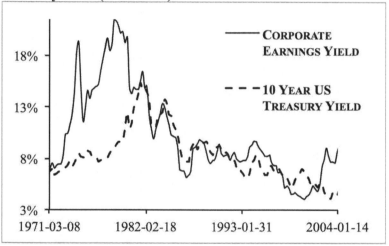

Note: Data adapted from Wilshire Associates® and Federal Reserve Bank of St. Louis (2017)[17, 4]

As you can see, since the bull market in US Treasuries began in 1981, stocks' earnings yields have generally moved in sync with US Treasury yields.

In this context, if bond yields are *falling* due to the Fed creating a bond bubble (pushing prices up forces yields down), then the ratio of stock earnings to stock prices needs to be falling as well. This means that either stocks earnings must fall or stock prices must rise.

However, because of the financial crisis and accompanying recession of 2008 to 2009, stock profits were generally *rising* on a year over year basis starting in 2009.

So stock earnings weren't falling… which meant that in order for the stock profits to stock prices ratio to fall along with US Treasury yields, **stock prices had to rise.**

Put simply, by pushing interest rates to extraordinary lows via ZIRP and monetary programs like QE, the Fed was indirectly *forcing* investors to buy stocks to seek significant returns. In this sense, the bond bubble directly fueled the stock bubble by forcing capital into riskier assets like stocks.

However, there was a second component here.

After the 2008 Crisis, individual investors were generally wary of stocks (why shouldn't they be, the market had just collapsed over 30% in a single year?). This meant a lack of buyers to force markets higher.

Enter the primary dealers.

Bernanke's Big Bank Bailout Bonanza

Remember from Chapter 2, *The Building of a Debt Mountain,* that when the US government issues new debt, a select group of the largest banks and financial institutions called primary dealers, are responsible for most of the purchases?

Well, guess whom the Fed was buying US Treasuries and other debts from via its QE programs and Operation Twist?

The primary dealers.

In this sense, QE 1 was a kind of backdoor bailout for these firms. The Fed bought their garbage mortgage-backed securities from them at 100 cents on the dollar giving them a fresh round of capital.

In contrast, QE 2 and Operation Twist were slightly different in that these programs gave the primary dealers the ultimate "dumb money" investor to front-run in the bond market for a quick profit.

However, ALL of the above programs accomplished ultimately the same thing: giving the primary dealers access to extra capital. Much of this new capital found its way into the stock market.

Chart 45 shows the Fed's balance sheet overlaid by a stock market index called the S&P 500. Note that as the Fed's balance sheet grew from acquiring assets, stocks rose in a virtual lock-stop. This became increasingly obvious as the Fed moved into "open ended" programs that ran continuously like QE 3.

Chart 45: Total Asssets Federal Reserve Banks, Billions US Dollars and S&P 500 Index (2009-2016).

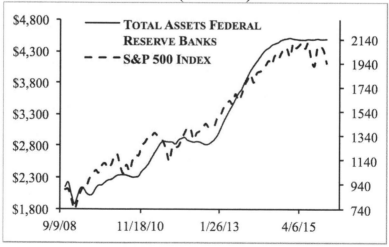

Note: Data adapted from Investing.com and Federal Reserve Bank of St. Louis (2017)[18]

In this sense, you could easily argue that the Fed's monetary programs directly inflated a bubble in stocks by providing a near continuous line of new capital to the big banks which then funneled this cash into stocks.

And, because these financial firms can leverage up to ten times their capital levels, stocks weren't the only asset class that benefitted from the Fed providing $3.5 trillion (the total dollar amount of Fed asset purchases) in capital to the primary dealers.

Why?

Because these firms aren't just primary dealers... they're also investment fund managers, brokers, and investment banks: the very firms responsible for directing capital throughout the financial system.

As a result of this, US stocks were not the only asset class to reflate courtesy of the bond bubble. Emerging market stocks, commodities, and the like all disconnected from economic fundamentals, fueled by the tsunami of Fed fueled liquidity.

In this sense Bernanke's bond bubble truly became the Everything Bubble: a situation in which the bedrock of the entire global financial system (US Treasuries) entered a bubble forcing all other asset classes to adjust accordingly.

Debt deflation had been conquered... for now. But, this bubble, like all bubbles, will one day burst. And when it does, it will make 2008 look like a picnic.

Good. God. Almighty.

PART 2:
What's To Come

CHAPTER 6:

REVIEW OF PART 1 AND INTRODUCTION TO PART 2

For those who decided to skip ahead to this section of the book, let's do a quick review of the first half. Even if you did read the last 100 pages, we've covered a lot of ground and it's worth condensing it into a simple outline.

The current US financial system was shaped via four key developments. They were:

1. The formation of the US Central Bank called the Federal Reserve or the Fed in 1913. This created a centralized banking system through which the flow of money and cost of money are controlled. The Fed also controls production of the US dollar though it is not actually a part of the US government.

2. Former President Franklin Delano Roosevelt began separating the US dollar from the Gold Standard in 1933. This began the process of making the US dollar a completely fiat currency or "paper money."

3. Former President Richard Nixon completely severed the US dollar from any link to gold in 1971. From this point onwards, the US began to issue debt aggressively as all debts would be paid with US dollars, which the Fed could print at any time.

4. Former Fed Chair Alan Greenspan's decision to ignore the United States growing mountain of debt for 19 years, leading to the current situation in which the Fed has no choice but to continually create asset bubbles (I call this situation the

"Era of Serial Bubbles") in order to stop debt deflation from collapsing the system when a crisis hits.

In pictorial form, since the United States completely abandoned the any link to gold in 1971, Chart 46 happened.

Chart 46: Total US Debt Securities and US Gross Domestic Product, Trillions US Dollars (1971-2016).

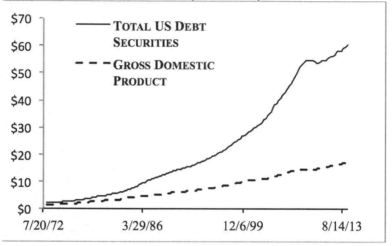

Note: Data adapted from Federal Reserve Bank of St. Louis (2017)[3]

As I noted in #4 in the list, because the US financial system is now completely saturated in debt, the Federal Reserve is forced to continuously create asset bubbles.

The problem with this (aside from the fact that it means the system moves from bubble to crisis every few years), is that the Fed has been forced to create <u>successive bubbles,</u> each time in a more senior asset class.

- 1996 to 2000 was the Tech Bubble or bubble in Technology stocks.

- 2003 to 2008 was the Housing Bubble: a bubble in US

real estate that became a global banking solvency crisis through the proliferation of Wall Street's unregulated derivatives products.

• 2009 to the present is the Bond Bubble or bubble in US sovereign bonds called Treasuries. And, because these bonds serve as the bedrock (the "risk free" rate of return) for the US financial system, once they went into a bubble, EVERYTHING went into a bubble, hence the term, *The Everything Bubble.*

This has brought the Fed to the End Game for Central Bank monetary policy. There is simply no other, more senior asset class the Fed can use to create another bubble when this one bursts.

Similarly, the Bond Bubble is too large for the Fed to truly contain when it pops. The US Tech Bubble was $7 trillion in size. The US Housing Bubble was $14 trillion in size.

The US Bond Bubble is $20 trillion in size. When you include junior debt instruments, it swells to over $60 trillion. And when you include derivatives associated with bond yields, it's over $124 trillion.

Put simply, the Bond Bubble is the largest asset bubble in history, in the senior-most asset class in the financial system. And, because these bonds serve as the benchmark for measuring all risk in the financial system, every asset class has become "bubbly" as a result of this.

So this is not merely a bubble in one asset class. It is truly the Everything Bubble. And, when it bursts the current US financial system will have to be restructured.

As a result of this, the Fed will be fighting tooth and nail to maintain the bond bubble at all costs. Over the coming months and years we will experience monetary policies that make even those from the period of 2009 to 2015 (a period in which the Fed cut interest rates to ZERO and spent over $3.5 trillion in Quantitative Easing) look relatively pedestrian.

Indeed, before the smoke clears on the Bond Bubble's bursting I expect to see the Fed:

1) Implement Negative Interest Rates Policy, or NIRP, well into the single digits (think rates of -3% or even -5% on bank accounts). This policy will be combined with nuclear levels of Quantitative Easing, or QE, to the tune of $100 billon or more per month.

2) Attempt a complete cash ban on large denominations of physical cash along with a carry tax (a process through which physical cash will be taxed) being placed on smaller bill denominations.

3) Implement numerous Bail-Ins through which savings deposits will be frozen and converted into a firm's equity, or simply seized in order to prop up failing banks and financial institutions.

If the above terms are unfamiliar to you, don't worry, we'll be covering all of them in great detail in the chapters ahead. For now, you can think of what's coming in these terms:

• There is too much debt in the US financial system.

• This debt can only continue to be serviced provided the Fed engages in extraordinary monetary policy.

• When the Bond Bubble begins to burst and debt deflation hits, the US government will sign off on the Fed implementing even MORE extraordinary policies designed to confiscate capital through interest rates, taxes, and Bail-Ins in order to prop up the system.

Before proceeding, I want to warn you that the bursting of the Bond Bubble will not come quickly. I am not predicting that this process will take a few months. It will take years and possibly even a decade.

There are two reasons for this.

The first concerns investor psychology and faith in the Fed's ability to maintain the system. The fact is that over the last 30+ years, investors have come to believe that there is no problem that the Fed cannot fix.

In the last 20 years alone, the US financial system has been affected by numerous global and domestic crises including the Mexican Peso Crisis (1994), the Asian Financial Crisis (1997), the Russian Ruble Crisis (1998), the Argentinian Crisis (1999-2002), the US Tech Crash (2000-2002), the US Housing Crash (2006-2008), the 2008 Global Financial Crisis (2008-2009), the Euro Banking Crisis (2010-2015) and more.

By hook or by crook, the Fed has managed to pull the US financial system back from the brink during all of these. As a result of this, an entire generation of investment professionals has grown middle aged, if not older, **without ever witnessing the Fed fail to contain a financial issue.**

Consider that the young man or woman who entered the investment community aged 22 in 1997, when the US entered the Era of Serial Bubbles, is now in his or her 40s, having never once experienced a financial crisis that wasn't immediately followed by the successful creation of another asset bubble.

Moreover, those investment professionals who *were* active even as young men or women during the last bear market in bonds (a time when debt grew increasingly more expensive to issue) are now at retirement age.

Indeed, to find a fund manager who was actively *managing money* for several years during the last bear market in bonds, you'd have to find someone who's 70+ years old… and still professionally active in the markets.

Because of this, when the Everything Bubble finally begins to burst, **it will take years for investment professionals to fully realize it and adjust accordingly.**

By way of example, let us consider the details surrounding the bursting of the Tech Bubble: the single largest stock market bubble of the last 100 years that we detailed in Chapter Three, *The Era of Serial Bubbles Begins.*

In this case, the bubble pertained to just one asset class (stocks). In fact, the bubble was relatively isolated to one specific sector: technology stocks.

And to top if off, it was absolutely obvious to anyone that it was a bubble (everyone except then-Fed Chairman Alan Greenspan, that is). You could literally know *nothing* about finance and look at a chart of the NASDAQ (a stock market focusing on tech stocks) and know that it wasn't going to end well (see Chart 47).

Chart 47: NASDAQ Composite Index (1990-2000).

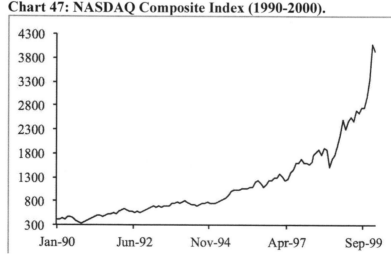

Note: Data adapted from NASDAQ OMX Group, Inc[10]

And yet, despite the fact that this bubble was absolutely obvious and involved only one asset class, it *still* took **professional investors** well over six months to realize that the bubble had burst.

Mind you, this wasn't just a six-month period in which stocks simply peaked and then remained at elevated levels; the market first experienced a MONSTROUS Crash during which it lost 20% of its value in the space of **two months.**

Yes, the market lost 1/5th of its value in just two months. But did that convince professional investors to start "selling the farm"? Nope. They continued to buy stocks at nearly every dip all the way down for over TWO YEARS.

Indeed, during a single six-month period in 2000, market pros saw stocks stage over 11 price moves greater than 8%. Keep in mind when looking at Chart 48 that all of these moves would have been considered *major.*

Chart 48: NASDAQ Composite Index (2000-2001).

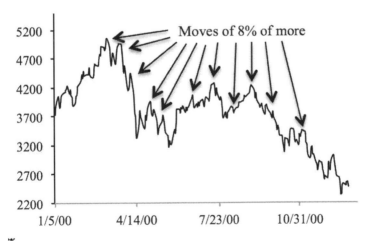

Note: Data adapted from NASDAQ OMX Group, Inc[10]

Put simply, stocks were clearly in a bubble. Indeed, it was THE

147

largest stock bubble in over 100 years based on numerous methods of valuing stocks. And yet, when it burst, there was no clear consensus even amongst professional investors as to where the market was heading.

My point with all of this is that even when an asset bubble is both very specific AND obvious, **the collapse is neither quick nor clean.**

So if the Tech Bubble took **three years** to bottom after bursting, you can be assured that the Bond Bubble or Everything Bubble will take considerably longer… and that's AFTER it bursts.

There is a second reason why the Everything Bubble will take a long time to collapse. It concerns the *political* implications of this particular bubble.

As I outlined in Chapter 2, *The Building of a Debt Mountain*, for 30+ years, the US government has been taking advantage of ever-cheaper debt to implement social programs and entitlement spending.

As a result, today more than 59% of the United States' federal budget goes towards some kind of social spending with roughly 49% of American households receiving some form of government assistance.

That comes to more than 150 million people.

In this environment, any politician who pushes to cut social spending is committing political suicide. Aside from angering potential voters, said politician is opening him- or herself to political attack from political opponents who are only too happy to point out how heartless he or she is to propose said cuts.

So do not expect the political class to permit the Everything Bubble to collapse without pushing for extreme measures.

Remember, back in 2008 when everyone thought the world was ending? As I've noted repeatedly throughout this book, the reality is that the amount of debt deflation that hit the system at that time was barely a blip in the US Debt Mountain.

And yet, this "blip" was so terrifying to the political class that politicians "signed off" on a level of intervention/ money printing that was absolutely staggering. During this brief period of debt deflation, lasting a total of 15 months, the following occurred:

- The Fed cut interest rates from 5.25-0.25% (September '07-December '08).

- The Bush Administration enacted the 2008 Economic Stimulus Act through which it mailed $100 billion in tax rebates to consumers (February '08).

- The Fed facilitated a deal to merge Bear Stearns with JP Morgan through which the Fed bought $30 billion worth of garbage mortgage derivatives (March '08).

- The Fed opened various lending windows to investment banks through which they could access capital directly from the Fed (March '08).

- The Treasury Department of the United States took a $400 billion stake in the mortgage giants Fannie and Freddie (September '08).

- The US government nationalized insurance giant AIG for $85 billion (September '08).

- The US government implemented a $25 billion automaker bailout (September '08).

- The US government spent $700 billion via the Troubled Assets Relief Program (TARP): a massive bank bailout to those firms with the greatest derivatives exposure on Wall Street (October '08).

- The Fed offered $540 billion to backstop money market funds (October '08).

- The Fed backstopped up to $280 billion of Citigroup's liabilities (October '08).

- The US government spent another $40 billion in bail-out money on AIG (November '08).

- The Fed announced QE 1, a program through which it would buy $600 billion in mortgage backed securities (November '08)

- The Fed backstopped up to $140 billion of Bank of America's liabilities (January '09)

- The Obama Administration enacted the American Recovery and Reinvestment Act of 2009, a stimulus program through which the US government spent $830 billion (February '09).

- The Fed expanded QE 1 by an additional $750 billion in debt purchases (March '09)

- The US Government spent $3 billion issuing rebates for automobile purchases via its Cash for Clunkers I & II programs (July-August '09)

At this point, we are told that the great recession officially ended and the United States entered a recovery. Despite this, the Fed kept interest rates at ZERO for another six years. It also spent an additional $600 billion buying debt securities via QE 2 (November '10), and another $1.8 trillion buying debt securities via QE 3 (launched September '12 and expanded December '12).

My point with the above overview is this: during the brief 15-month period of debt deflation, the political and financial elite spent a truly staggering amount of money via over a dozen major interventions combating the bursting of the Housing Bubble.

And that bubble was *significantly smaller* than the Everything Bubble of today!

So when the Everything Bubble finally bursts, the political class will be pushing hard for the Fed to engage in even more extreme monetary policies. I believe that these policies will include:

1) The Fed cutting interest rates below zero into negative territory (think of being charged -3% or even -5% on bank accounts). The goals here would be:

   a. To prop up the US Debt Mountain by charging interest on debt holders (think of this as a kind of government "Bail-In" via the bond markets).

   b. To force "money on the sidelines" to move into risk assets to stop the debt bubble from deflating (if rates fall low enough, savers will be forced to move their money into bonds and stocks).

2) The Fed and the political elite will push for, and likely, implement a cash ban on large bill denominations of physical cash as well as a carry tax (a process through which physical cash will be taxed) on smaller bill denominations.

   This will be sold as an attempt to crack down on money laundering or some other illicit activity. However, the goal here is actually to "lock in" depositors so they cannot escape the impact of the afore-mentioned negative rates.

3) The Fed and other financial regulators will implement numerous "Bail-Ins": a process through which savings deposits will be frozen and converted into firm equity or simply seized in order to prop up failing banks and financial institutions.

4) This will go hand in hand with a global wealth tax in which deposits over a certain threshold will be "taxed." Again, this will be sold as an attempt to crack down on "tax evasion", or some such illicit activity, but the goal is to seize capital to prop up insolvent financial institutions.

151

Over the next 60 pages we'll explore all of these policies in detail. Depending on when you read this book, this process may or may not have started. So the following chapters will provide a road map for understanding where we are in the process as well as what's to come.

Let's dive in.

CHAPTER 7:
NIRP AND NUCLEAR LEVELS OF QE

First and foremost, when the Everything Bubble bursts, the Fed will turn to the same policies it used to address the Housing Crash, only on a more extreme basis.

This means the Fed will be:

1) Cutting the Fed's Target Federal Funds Rate to new lows.

2) Implementing large-scale purchases of debt and other securities via Quantitative Easing or QE.

Regarding #1, as we discussed in Chapter 5, *The Everything Bubble,* the Fed controls the "cost" of money in the financial system via its Target Federal Funds Rate.

This is one of the primary tools the Fed uses to generate bubbles. By keeping rates below the pace of US economic growth for prolonged periods, the Fed effectively makes money "free" in that borrowers can borrow money and then invest it in virtually anything related to economic growth for a profit.

This is the *literal* recipe for bubbles. And the Fed has *intentionally* done this twice since the United States reached the point of debt saturation in the mid-'90s:

> • From 2001 until 2005, to combat the Tech Crash, the Fed kept its Federal Funds Rate well below the pace of US economic growth to create the Housing Bubble.

> • From 2008 until 2016, to combat the Housing Crash, the Fed kept its Federal Funds Rate well below the pace of economic growth to create the Bond Bubble, which I call the Everything Bubble.

In pictorial form, we're talking about the Fed doing Chart 49.

Chart 49: Effective Federal Funds Rate and Year Over Year US Gross Domestic Product Growth (2000-2016).

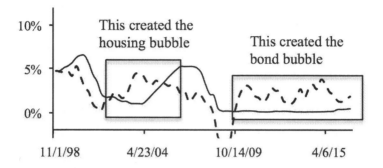

Note: Data adapted from Federal Reserve Bank of St. Louis (2017)[3,11]

Looking at Chart 49, the first thing that jumps out is that with each successive crisis, the Fed has been forced to engage in ever more extreme rate cuts in order to generate the desired effect (another bubble).

For instance, in the aftermath of the Tech Crash, the Fed cut rates from **6.4% to a low of 1%** where they remained just **12 months** before the Fed starting hiking rates.

By way of contrast, in the aftermath of the Housing Crash, the Fed cut rates from **5.26% to a low of 0.25%** where they remained for **seven years.**

See for yourself in Chart 50.

Chart 50: Fed Rate Cut Depth and Duration in Response to Tech Crash and Housing Crash.

Fed Actions	Previous Rate Peak	Cut Rates to a Low Of	Rates Held at Low For
In Response to Tech Crash	6.50%	1.00%	12 months
In Response to Housing Crash	5.25%	0.15%	84 months

Note: Data adapted from Federal Reserve Bank of St. Louis (2017)[11]

Note how extreme Fed rate policy became in response to the Housing Crash. For those of you who are visual, below is the historical chart of the Effective Federal Funds Rate running back to the mid-'50s. As you can see, the Fed's implementation of Zero Interest Rate Policy or ZIRP was a truly *EXTREME* policy (see Chart 51).

Chart 51: Effective Federal Funds Rate (1954-2016).

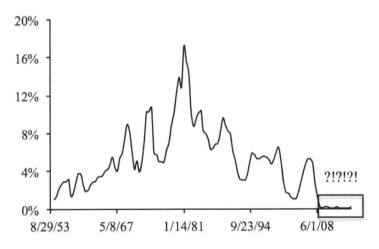

Note: Data adapted from Federal Reserve Bank of St. Louis (2017)[11]

This begs the question… just how extreme will Fed interest rate policy have to become when the Everything Bubble bursts?

When the Everything Bubble bursts, the Fed will be forced to cut interest rates into NEGATIVE territory… meaning rates through-out the financial system (including the rates paid on your savings deposits) will go *negative*.

And the Fed won't simply be flirting with this policy; **before the smoke clears, I expect the Fed's Target Federal Funds Rate to be at -3%, if not -5%.**

Before you label me as insane, consider that the policies the Fed employed in response to the Housing Crash (seven years of ZIRP and $3.5 trillion in QE) would have sounded completely insane back in 2003 or 2004.

However, using the 2008 Crisis as justification, the Fed was able to implement both of those policies with little political fallout. Indeed, if anything, numerous individuals within the political/ financial elite were berating the Fed for not doing more!

So while rates of -3% or -5% might sound insane right now, wait until the Everything Bubble bursts, and I guarantee you that we'll be hearing calls for Negative Interest Rate Policy (NIRP) from politicians, financial leaders, and the media around the clock.

Let me explain…

The Political Consequences of a Sovereign Debt Crisis

As I outlined in Chapter 2, *The Building of a Debt Mountain*, over the last 30+ years, the US government has relied extensively on debt issuance to fund its ever-growing list of entitlements/ social spending.

Because US Treasuries have been in a bull market (meaning interest rates were continuously falling and debt was getting cheaper to issue), the US government's policy of spending more than it takes in via taxes has been relatively easy to maintain.

The bursting of the Everything Bubble would end all of this.

156

Consider the following...

In 2016, the average interest rate the United States paid on its debt was only 1.9%. As a result of this, interest payments on the federal debt only comprised 7% of the federal budget.

Even with debt payments requiring so little money on a relative basis, because of the United States' massive entitlement spending, the Federal Government still ran a deficit of roughly half a trillion dollars (meaning it spent roughly $500 billion more than it brought in via taxes).

That ~$500 billion was funded via... you guessed it, debt issuance.

So what happens if the Everything Bubble bursts, debt deflation hits US Treasuries, and the United States' debt payments explode higher as it is forced to pay an average interest rate of 5% or 6% on its already $20+ trillion in debt?

Game Over.

Remember, the United States government is already spending more than it takes in via taxes. So it would have to fund any increase in debt payments by issuing *more* debt.

But in the context of the bursting of the Everything Bubble, this would be all but impossible. Remember, when the Everything Bubble bursts, the US sovereign bond market will enter debt deflation, meaning it's getting *more* difficult and *more* expensive for the United States to issue debt.

So issuing more debt to cover ballooning debt payments wouldn't solve the problem. Assuming the United States was even able to issue debt during an episode of debt deflation, doing so would only make things worse on a fiscal basis.

This would leave only three options for the US government:

1) Raise taxes aggressively (to increase revenues, reduce the deficit, and pay the debt).

2) Begin cutting entitlements aggressively (to reduce the budget and free up money to pay the debt).

3) Default on the debt, causing a systemic implosion (think of a crisis exponentially greater than that of 2008).

All three of these options represent political suicide: **no politician is going to push for raising taxes, cutting social spending, or letting the United States default on its debts.**

Thus there is really only one option...the Fed would have to intervene aggressively in the bond markets to attempt to reflate the Bond Bubble.

And since it took seven years of Zero Interest Rate Policy (ZIRP) and $3.5 trillion in QE to reflate the financial system following the housing crash, the Fed will be forced to engage in even more extreme monetary policy to deal with the Bond Bubble's collapse.

This will eventually lead to the Fed employing Negative Interest Rate Policy (NIRP) and massive QE programs of $100+, if not $200+ billion per month.

Let's tackle each of these.

NIRP: Tackling the Short-End of the Bond Market

As I noted in Chapter 5, *The Everything Bubble*, short-term Treasuries track the Fed's Target Federal Funds Rate. So, if the Fed cuts its Target Federal Funds Rate to negative, **short-term Treasury yields will follow suit.**

Yes, that means that bond investors will be *paying* the US government for the right to lend it money.

I realize that this flies in the face of common sense.

Common sense dictates that if a Central Bank were to cut rates to negative, investors would dump the bonds. After all, who in his or her right mind is willing to be CHARGED for lending out money?

Well, when it comes to sovereign bond markets, the reality is that virtually *EVERYONE* is willing to PAY the government for the right to lend it money… **provided the alternative is systemic collapse.**

If you don't believe me, consider what happened in Europe a few years ago.

Europe: a Case Study in NIRP and Nuclear QE

From 2010-2014, various European member states, specifically the troubled nations of Portugal, Ireland, Italy, Greece, and Spain (collectively these were referred to, unflatteringly, as the PIIGS nations) experienced intense episodes of debt deflation.

During these episodes, prices of the sovereign bonds for all of these countries collapsed, pushing their respective yields higher.

As a general rule of thumb, when the yield on a given country's 10-Year Government Bond hits 7%, the country is deemed insolvent. As you can see in Chart 52, the yields on Italy and Spain's 10-Year Government Bonds hit these thresholds in 2011 and 2012, respectively.

Chart 52: Yields on Italy's and Spain's 10-Year Government Bonds (2009-2013).

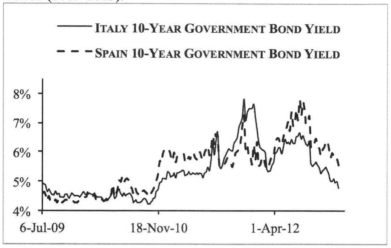

Note: Data adapted from Investing.com (2017)[19]

Now, debt deflation for the sovereign bonds of any nation tends to be catastrophic. But for members of the European Union (or EU) it was a financial death sentence: only the European Central Bank or ECB can print Euros, so when an individual European member state gets into a fiscal mess, it *cannot* print its way out via currency depreciation.

Moreover, the ECB can't just "gift" Euros to individual member states, either. For one thing, doing so would violate the European Union's charter. And even if the ECB *did* gift a handout to an individual member state, it would only trigger a different type of crisis, as every other indebted EU member (read: *all* of them) would line up asking for one as well.

So to deal with this situation, the ECB, working with the EU, first engaged in bailouts (effectively emergency loans made in exchange for the promise of financial austerity).

When this didn't work, the ECB turned to… NIRP and QE.

The immediate implication of this was that going forward, any-one who loaned money to an EU member state for a short period of time (like the United States, EU members issue debt for peri-ods as short as a few weeks) **would end up paying that country for the right to do so.**

Now, common logic would dictate that this would lead to inves-tors dumping the PIIGS' sovereign bonds. After all, if you were already concerned that a nation is heading towards bankruptcy, why would you even think about earning less in exchange for lending it money, let along *paying it* for the right to do so?

Instead, the exact opposite happened: instead of dumping the PI-IGS' sovereign bonds, investors actually *piled into* these bonds, forcing their yields to record lows.

The ECB then proceeded to cut rates deeper into NIRP three more times. And with each additional cut, yields on PIIGS' sov-ereign bonds fell further until, in 2015, investors began PAYING these countries for the right to lend them money in the short-term.

You can see this insanity playing out in Spain's and Italy's 3-Month Government Bonds in Chart 53.

Chart 53: Yields on Italy and Spain's 3-Month Government Bonds (2014-2016).

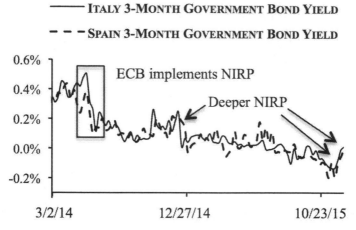

Note: Data adapted from Investing.com (2017)[20]

But wait, it gets even crazier for those EU members like Germany that were in somewhat better financial condition than the PIIGS. In response to NIRP, German Government Bonds rallied so aggressively that their yields were even MORE negative than the ECB's official rate policy!

Put another way, investors were willing to PAY Germany for the right to lend it money even MORE than the ECB's official NIRP policy warranted! You can see this insanity in Chart 54.

Chart 54: ECB Interest Rate and German 3-Month Government Bond Yield (2014-2016).

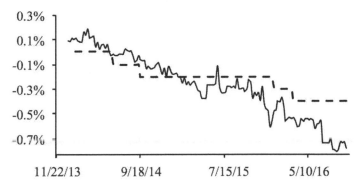

──── GERMAN 3-MONTH GOVERNMENT BOND YIELD

‒ ‒ ‒ ECB INTEREST RATE

Note: Data adapted from Investing.com and European Central Bank (2017)[21]

How is this possible?

Remember from Chapter 5, *The Everything Bubble*, that when a Central Bank implements a large Quantitative Easing (QE) program, it is effectively providing the ultimate "dumb money" buyer to the bond markets: a buyer who literally broadcasts in advance when he would be buying bonds and that he would not be picky about price.

Well, when the ECB began to cut rates to negative in 2014, it *also* began talking about implementing a massive QE program (even though the legality of such a program was still questionable at the time). And, when I saw massive, I mean *massive*, as in €1 trillion.

Investors took this to signify that the ECB would be backstopping the European bond markets **no matter what** and acted accordingly (piled into EU member state bonds).

163

After all, what choice did they really have? The alternative was a debt-deflation induced systemic collapse in which entire countries went bust (along with all of the big European banks that were the largest owners of EU member states' sovereign debts).

Put simply, when the alternative means, "losing everything," just about everybody is willing to "lose a little" via NIRP.

I have little doubt that a similar situation will unfold in the United States when the Fed is forced to cut rates into negative territory to combat its own deflating Bond Bubble.

For certain, the political class in the United States would embrace this policy as maintaining the Bond Bubble would allow the US government to continue to fund its massive entitlement/social spending programs.

Large financial firms and banks would also embrace this policy given that the alternative would mean imploding (all the large banks use US Treasuries as the ultimate collateral backstopping their massive derivatives portfolios).

But what about the United States population… will Americans go along with being *charged* for keeping their money in a bank via NIRP?

Again, the answer here is contextual: the Fed will only be able to implement NIRP in the context of a MAJOR crisis and economic contraction. As the Housing Crash and 2008 crisis made clear, when the financial system is under duress, the Fed can get away with just about anything with little political fallout.

Moreover, when the coming Bond Crash hits and debt deflation sets in, it's not going to be confined to US sovereign bonds; it's going to hit any and all debt in the US financial system including the $3.8+ trillion in consumer credit owed by Americans. Between student loans, auto-loans, credit card debt, and the like, the

American population will be *highly* in favor of anything that will force rates lower to reduce their debt payments.

The question then becomes, *"how low will rates go?"*

Rates Are Going to -3%, if not -5%

As we discussed earlier in this chapter, with each successive crisis, the Fed has been forced to cut rates deeper.

- During the Tech Crash, the Fed cut rates from **6.4% to a low of 1%**.
- During the Housing Crash, the Fed cut rates from **5.26% to a low of 0.25%**.

You'll note that in both instances, the Fed cut rates by roughly 5% or so. It turns out this is roughly the norm for Fed activity during recessions/ crises. Chart 55 is a table outlining previous rate cutting cycles and their causes running back to the 1950s.

Chart 55: History of Fed Rate Cuts in Response to Crises/ Recessions (1957-2009)

	Previous Rate Peak	Rates Cut to a Low Of	Total Cuts
Recession (Oct '57 to May '58)	3.50%	0.63%	2.87%
Recession (August' 69 Feb '71)	9.19%	3.72%	5.47%
Inflationary Recession (Nov '73 to May '75)	12.92%	5.22%	7.70%
Inflationary Recession (Jan '80 to July '80)	17.61%	9.03%	8.58%
Recession (July '81 to Feb '83)	19.04%	8.51%	10.53%
Recession (July '90 to Mar '91)	8.15%	2.92%	5.23%
Recession (Feb '01 to Jan '02)	6.50%	1.73%	4.77%
Recession (Nov '07 to July '09)	4.49%	0.15%	4.34%
		Average Total Rate Cut	6.19%

Note: Data adapted from Federal Reserve Bank of St. Louis (2017)[11]

For clarity's sake, I'm using the previous rate peak regardless of whether rates were at that level when the recession official-ly began or not (the Fed typically starts cutting rates before a recession is officially declared). And as we've noted previously, the Fed will often continue to cut rates even after the recession is "officially" over; so the rate "low" might actually happen *after* the recession is finished.

Regardless, the key point is that on average the Fed cuts rates by a total of 5-6% when dealing with significant economic or financial problems. So you can expect rates to drop 5%-6% from their previous peak whenever the Bond Bubble bursts.

So, if rates are at 3% when the Bond Bubble bursts and the crisis begins, you can expect rates to bottom at NIRP of -2% or -3%.

And, if rates are at 1% when the Bond Bubble bursts and the crisis begins, you can expect rates to bottom at NIRP of -4% or -5%.

This is particularly true given the magnitude of the crisis the financial system will be facing. I fully expect that before the smoke clears, the "cost of money" via the Fed's Target Federal Funds Rate will be -3%, if not -5%.

Again, I realize this sounds impossible now. But, seven years of ZIRP and $3.5 trillion in QE sounded impossible back in 2003.

Speaking of which, when the Everything Bubble bursts, I also expect the Fed to unleash a truly massive QE program of $100+ or even $200+ billion per month.

This policy, combined with NIRP, will represent the Fed's attempt to backstop the entire bond market. But it will also open the door to the ultimate bailout: a situation in which the Fed pays the US' public debt payments itself.

Buckle up. We're about to get truly crazy.

NIRP+ Nuclear Levels of QE= the Fed Pays The United States' Debt Itself

As we outlined in Chapter 5, *The Everything Bubble*, Quantitative Easing or QE is the process through which the Fed prints *new* money to buy assets, usually debt securities.

When the Housing Bubble burst, the Fed "spent" roughly $3.5 trillion doing this over the course of six years. And, at the peak of its QE programs in 2013, the Fed was "spending" $80 billion per month buying assets via QE programs.

With that in mind, I fully expect that when the Everything Bubble bursts, the Fed will be announcing large-scale, if not NUCLEAR, levels of QE to drive down the long-end of the Treasury market.

When I say "NUCLEAR," I mean $100+ billion per month, and possibly as much as $250 billion per month.

Here's how it will work.

Remember from Chapter 2, *The Building of a Debt Mountain*, when we talk about US sovereign bonds or Treasuries, we're actually talking about a range of debt instruments that mature over different time periods, ranging from four weeks to 30 years.

As we've already covered, the short-end of the Treasury market is comprised of T-Bills that mature anywhere between four weeks and one year. These bonds track the Fed's Target Federal Funds Rate as illustrated in Chart 56.

Chart 56: Effective Federal Funds Rate and 3-Month US Treasury Bill Yield (2006-2012).

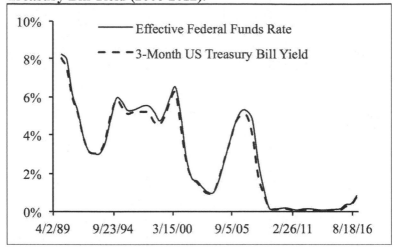

Note: Data adapted from Federal Reserve Bank of St. Louis (2017)[11, 14]

So, implementing NIRP will drag down the short-end of the bond market.

But what about the long-end of the bond market? How will the Fed get long-term Treasuries to follow short-term T-Bills down the NIRP rabbit hole?

Quantitative Easing, or QE. And not just a little… a LOT.

To deal with the Housing Crash, the Fed implementing QE programs, usually to the tune of $25 billion to $80 billion per month.

With that in mind, when the Everything Bubble bursts I expect the Fed to announce QE programs focusing on buying long-term Treasuries to the tune of $100+ billion per month (along with other QE programs to buy other assets, as we'll cover shortly).

Doing this would:

1) Provide banks/ financial firms/ bond investors with "easy money" in the form of front-running the "dumb money buyer" provided by the Fed via the QE program.

2) Drive down long-term Treasuries, allowing bond investors to offset the losses from negative yields with gains from bonds rising in price (remember when yields fall, bond prices rise and bond investors profit from capital gains).

3) **Allow the Fed to make the US debt payments itself.**

Wait... what?

Think of it this way...

> • With negative interest rates, the person who is *BUYING* US sovereign debt is PAYING the United States (rather than the other way around).
>
> • With massive QE programs in place, the Fed will be the "person" who is buying most of the US debt (more on this shortly) and therefore is responsible for paying the United States the amount required via the negative yield.
>
> • The Fed controls the printing press that prints US dollars.

Remember, from Chapter 2, *The Building of a Debt Mountain,* once then-President Richard Nixon completely severed the US dollar from the Gold Standard, the United States would be paying all of its debts *exclusively* in US dollars, that the Fed could print at anytime.

With negative interest rates forcing lenders to pay the United States to own its bonds, and QE programs leading to the Fed acquiring the bulk of US Treasuries, we'd actually reach the point through which the Fed would be *actively printing money* to finance US debt payments itself.

This would represent the End Game for Fed policy: a situation in which the Fed would acquire most if not all new debt issuance from the United States (usually by buying it from financial firms that would be front-running the Fed's QE programs) and then printing new money to pay the interest on the negative yields.

Put simply, **NIRP+ Nuclear Levels of QE= the Fed Covers US Debt Payments Itself.**

The political class will love this because it means the US government can continue to spend money it doesn't have.

Financial firms will tolerate this because the alternative means blowing up their derivatives portfolios and becoming the next Lehman Brothers.

And Americans will tolerate it because the alternative means interest payments soaring on consumer debt.

I realize all of this sounds completely insane, but I can assure you that this scheme will work for a time, as it will be the proverbial "only game in town." When the Everything Bubble bursts, this scheme, as insane as it sounds right now, will look relatively sane.

Indeed, Japan's been running a similar scheme for well over a decade.

The Single Biggest Investor in Japan's Bond Market and Stock Market Is... Japan's Central Bank

Before we delve into the insanity of Japan's current central bank policy, you first need a little background.

Back in the 1980s, Japan experienced a truly massive credit (debt) bubble.

To give you an idea of just how excessive things became, at one point the land under the Emperor's Palace (roughly 1.3 square miles) was considered to be worth more than ALL of the real estate in the State of California combined.

So when I say that Japan experienced a massive debt bubble, I really do mean MASSIVE.

This bubble burst, as all bubbles do, in the early '90s. And at that time Japan's Central Bank (called the Bank of Japan or BoJ) had a choice:

1) Let the entire financial system collapse, clear the bad debts, and then start over, or…

2) Attempt to backstop the debt markets via ZIRP and QE.

The Bank of Japan chose option #2, cutting interest rates to zero or ZIRP in 1999 and launching its first QE program in 2000. It then maintained both for five years (truth be told, it maintained ZIRP for 16 years, but we'll get to that in a moment).

The Bank of Japan soon found out what the United States Federal Reserve would later discover in 2010: that while ZIRP and QE are not very good at generating economic growth, **they're absolutely fantastic for maintaining a debt bubble.**

And, since this was effectively "the only game in town" (no one wanted to be responsible for letting the system truly collapse, even if that might present the only method of clearing the bad debts out and setting the stage for sustained economic growth) the political and financial elites signed off on it.

Since that time, the Bank of Japan has dealt with any and all issues by implementing more massive QE programs.

Japan wants to issue more debt to try and "spend" its way into growth?

Buy the debt with QE.

Japanese stocks aren't rallying any more and investors are getting nervous again?

Buy Japanese stocks (via various investment funds) with QE.

QE isn't working as well as the Bank of Japan hoped?

Expand QE by printing even more money and buying even more assets.

Even that doesn't seem to be working anymore?

You guessed it… MORE QE… and try NIRP.

If you think I'm being facetious here, consider the following…

Japan's sovereign Debt to GDP ratio first cleared 100% in the mid-'90s. At this level, a nation is usually considered to be bankrupt (meaning that it is HIGHLY unlikely it will ever pay its debt back) and bonds investors start its dumping bonds.

Not with Japan.

Because the Bank of Japan was ready to buy the nation's debt by the truckload, the bonds markets have given Japan a "pass"… and not just for a little while, **for well over 16 years.**

As a result of this, Japan now has a sovereign Debt to GDP ratio of well over 230%, and there's no sign of it stopping any time soon. Indeed, as of 2016, the Bank of Japan was buying up some 50% of Japan's new debt issuance.

Let me repeat that.

In 2016, Japan issued roughly $750 billion worth of debt.

The Bank of Japan bought HALF of it.

And no one blinked.

But wait… it gets even crazier.

Remember how I mentioned that the Bank of Japan was *also* using QE to buy stocks (albeit via various investment funds)?

As of 2016, the Bank of Japan had bought so many stocks that **it was the single largest shareholder for one quarter of Japan's 225 largest publicly traded companies.**

Yes, the #1 owner of Japan's debt AND its stock market… is the Bank of Japan.

And somehow it's worked.

Indeed, some of the smartest hedge fund managers in the world have gone bust trying to bet on Japan's collapse. Shorting Japanese Government Bonds (betting that the Bank of Japan would fail and debt deflation would take hold) has proven to be so disastrous that this trade is famously called "the widow maker."

This is why I believe the US Federal Reserve will be able to get away with a similar scheme, at least for a time. In fact, because the US Federal Reserve is in charge of printing the US dollar (the reserve currency of the world), I believe it will be able to get away with even more extreme measures.

After all, if the Bank of Japan can buy HALF of Japan's annual debt issuance and be the largest shareholder for a quarter of Japan's largest companies without the markets saying *"sorry guys,*

173

this is too much," what can the US Federal Reserve, the single most important central bank in the world get away with?

NIRP and NUCLEAR QE.

So… just how much QE are we talking about?

The Fed Will Be the Second Or Third Largest "Country" in the World

Back in 2000, when the Bank of Japan announced its first QE program, the bank's balance sheet was a mere 14% of Japan's Gross Domestic Product.

Now thanks to nearly two decades of QE, the Bank of Japan's balance sheet has ballooned up to an incredible 90% of Japan's Gross Domestic Product. Put simply, the Bank of Japan is now nearly the size of Japan's **entire annual economic output (see Chart 57)!**

Chart 57: Bank of Japan Balance Sheet as a Percentage of Japan Gross Domestic Product (2006-2016).

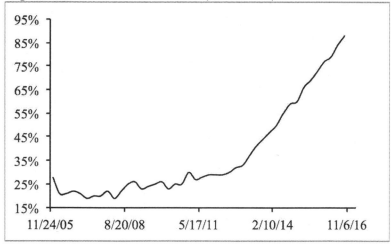

Note: Data adapted from OECD.org[22]

Now, I wouldn't go so far as to claim the US Federal Reserve will be able to pull off a similar balance sheet expansion (for one thing, the world is a lot further down the monetary rabbit hole today than it was in 1999).

However, the Fed has already performed a major balance sheet expansion since 2008. Thanks to QE, the Fed's balance sheet has grown from a mere 6% of US Gross Domestic Product in 2008 to roughly 27% of US Gross Domestic Product where it stands today (see Chart 58).

Chart 58: US Federal Reserve Balance Sheet as a Percentage of US Gross Domestic Product (2008-2016).

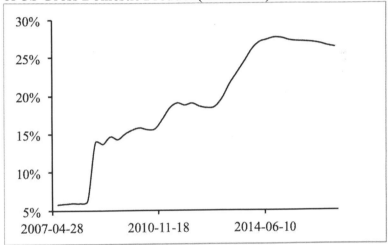

Note: Data adapted from Federal Reserve Bank of St. Louis (2017)[18, 3]

Given the magnitude of the Everything Bubble, we can **at least** expect the Fed to double its balance sheet from the peak established in response to the Housing Crash. This would mean the Fed balance sheet growing to 50% of US Gross Domestic Product.

Here's how it would work.

To date, the single largest QE program the Fed has engaged in was QE 3. During this program the Fed was printing roughly $80 billion in new money per month for a period of roughly two years.

When the bond bubble bursts, we can expect the Fed to do ***at least*** TWICE this rate of purchases for ***at least*** as long. This would mean the Fed printing at least $160 billion <u>per month</u> for twenty four months or a total of $3.8 TRILION in QE in the span of two years.

Based on current levels, this would bring the Fed's balance sheet to nearly $8 trillion or a little under 45% of the US Gross Domestic Product. At that level, if the Fed was its own country **<u>it would be the second or third largest country in the world.</u>**

Again, if this seems insane, consider that the Bank of Japan has been able to get away with a balance sheet expansion far greater than this for 16 years and:

1) It wasn't facing a sovereign bond crisis during this expansion.

2) It doesn't control the printing of the reserve currency of the world (the US dollar).

Again, it all boils down to this… when the Everything Bubble bursts, it will be because the bond markets begin to doubt that the United States will be able to pay its debts.

When this happens, the Fed will be the proverbial "only game in town" as it is forced to choose:

1) Let the Everything Bubble collapse, clear out the bad debt, and reset the entire financial system (this option also involves everyone in leadership roles at the Fed losing their jobs), or…

2) Cut rates to negative, engage in nuclear QE (monetize everything) and have the Fed pay the US debt directly.

I can assure you, the Fed won't be opting for option #1. Since 1987, the Fed has dealt with every financial issue by hitting the "print" button on the US dollar and cutting interest rates. And since 1996, each successive crisis has been handled via ever more extraordinary monetary policies.

So, the Fed isn't going to suddenly "get religion" when the Everything Bubble goes.

At the very least, we can expect the Fed to engage in monetary policy twice of that which it used in the aftermath of the Housing Crash (ZIRP and QE programs of $80 billion per month and ZIRP).

However, even more extreme policies are not out of the question.

This will ultimately result in QE programs of **at least $100 billion per month** combined with Negative Interest Rate Policy or NIRP of -3% to -5%.

This will force both the short-end and the long-end of the bond market down and create a situation in which the Fed itself will be paying the US government's debt payments via more money printing.

As far as the Fed will be concerned, the only negative to this will be the fact that cutting rates to negative 3% or negative 5% will be politically toxic after a time as it means Americans would be CHARGED to keep their money in the banks.

"Wait a minute", you might be thinking, *"if the Fed wants to CHARGE me to keep my money in a bank, I'll just take my money out and put it in a safe."*

Enter a cash ban.

CHAPTER 8:
THE WAR ON CASH

As we covered in the last chapter, when the Everything Bubble bursts, the US Federal Reserve will begin cutting its Target Federal Funds Rate and engaging in large scale Quantitative Easing (or QE) programs.

Eventually this will result in the Fed cutting rates into negative territory (the famed Negative Interest Rate Policy or NIRP) while printing $100+ billion per month in new money and using it to buy assets (bonds and other debts) from banks and other financial firms.

The purpose of these policies will be to reflate the US sovereign bond market. However, both policies will have secondary effects on the US financial system.

NIRP, in particular, will be a game changer as eventually it will lead to US banks cutting their deposit rates (what they pay depositors on their savings accounts) into negative territory as well.

Yes, I'm talking about banks CHARGING you for the right to keep YOUR money there.

The Fed will present this situation as a case of it employing extraordinary measures to stop the US financial system from collapsing. However, the reality is that NIRP is part of a larger campaign by the Fed and financial regulators to force you and I to move our capital out of cash and into risk assets like stocks and bonds, thereby helping to reflate the financial system.

I call this campaign "The War on Cash." And believe me, it will be a war.

Why? What's so terrible about cash that the Fed wants to declare war on it?

The answers to those questions depend on whom you ask. To you or me, cash is money or wealth. To the Fed, cash is a **major problem.**

As we outlined in Chapter 1, *How Debt Became Money*, when then-President Richard Nixon completely severed the US dollar from any link to gold in 1971, the US dollar became a completely free-floating currency.

Put simply, cash ceased to be "hard" money or money that was backed by something. Therefore it no longer maintained its purchasing power or "value," so to speak.

Instead, cash became just another asset class like stocks or bonds: something that can rise or fall in value depending on how the financial system is functioning relative to various factors (inflation, economic growth, etc.).

However, there's one key difference between cash and every other asset class.

When an investor buys stocks, bonds, real estate, commodities, etc… he or she is *helping* to inflate the financial system. As we've covered extensively, the Fed loves this because it means your capital is helping to push these asset prices higher, which helps avert the dreaded debt deflation the Fed wants to avoid at all costs.

In contrast, when an investor "buys" cash (by selling stocks, bonds or some other asset class) he or she is *deflating* asset prices and by extension, the financial system. Yes, the dreaded "D" word that the Fed fears.

And, if too many investors sell assets/ buy cash, it can cause a crash in the financial markets. Indeed, this is precisely what triggered the 2008 meltdown, as we will discuss shortly.

As far as the Fed is concerned, that's reason enough to hate cash as an asset class.

However, there's a second, even more dangerous component to cash, particularly *physical cash*. You might find this hard to believe, but physical money (as in coins and bills) is in fact a *systemic risk* for the Fed.

To understand what I mean by this, you first need to understand how the US financial system is structured based on different categories of "money."

The following is a technical breakdown of the different categories of "money" in the US financial system. If you are not interested in these details and simply want to continue on to how the Fed will be implementing its War on Cash, skip ahead to the section titled *Too Much Money Moving to Cash= Crashes or Systemic Risk.*

99% of "Money" Is Just Electrons Stored In a Bank Server

Let's talk about money.

Collectively, there is about $117 TRILLION in wealth in the US financial system.

Of this, only $13.5 trillion is stored in cash (as opposed to shares in a stock, Treasury security, or some other asset that would have to be sold to become cash).

And of that $13.5 trillion in cash, only $1.5 trillion is in the form of **physical coins and bills**.

That is correct, out of all the wealth in the Unites States, just a little over 1% is in actual physical "money" you can hold in your hand. The rest is in the form of electrons stored somewhere in a bank server or a brokerage account.

I've illustrated this in a pie chart (see Chart 59).

Chart 59: Physical Cash Vs. Total Wealth in the US Financial System.

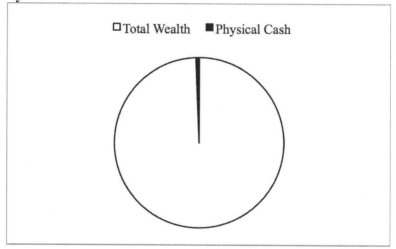

□Total Wealth   ■Physical Cash

Note: Data adapted from Federal Reserve Bank of St. Louis (2017)[23]

Note how small the "physical cash" slice is in that pie: the black sliver is *barely* visible at first glance.

This is intentional.

Remember, the original reason the Federal Reserve banking system was created was to stop another 1907-style banking crisis from ever happening again.

By quick way of review, that crisis was caused by *unregulated* banks making excessive loans (meaning they didn't have enough capital on hand to stay in business if a significant portion of these loans defaulted).

To stop a repeat of this mess, after the Federal Reserve banking system was established in 1913, every bank that was granted a federal charter to operate in the United States was REQUIRED by law to join the Fed's banking system.

Indeed, even those banks or institutions that are not granted federal banking charters (state banks or credit unions) are *still* subject to the Federal Reserve banking system's regulations. And they are connected to the Fed via its payment services system (the means through which money flows through the US financial system).

The idea here was that in this fashion every bank/ financial institution would be in some way, "connected" to the Fed so that it had access to capital if another systemic crisis hit.

The flip side of this is that in our current US financial system, **money, rarely, if ever, leaves the Federal Reserve banking system; instead it just flows from one bank account (connected to the Fed) to another.**

Back in the day, this meant physical checks being sent to a Federal Reserve Regional Bank that acted as a clearinghouse with the ability to move money from one bank to another. Today, it means money moving electronically through the Federal Reserve payment system.

Let me give you an example. Let's say you go to the store and buy a gallon of milk using your checking card.

When you "accept" the purchase on the card terminal at the store's register, three things happen:

1) The store's electronic payment system removes the funds from your personal bank account. This transaction is

usually listed as "pending" until it clears.

2) The Fed payment system begins the process of depositing those same funds in the store's business account at its bank (again the funds will be listed as "pending" until the transaction clears).

3) The card company you used (Visa, MasterCard, or whatever) takes a small fee from the the transaction and begins depositing it into the card company's business account at its own bank.

This sounds like money is moving around a lot, doesn't it? But the reality is that ALL of these transactions involve money flowing through the Fed's payment system.

On top of this, every bank involved in these transactions (your bank, the store's bank, and the payment processor's bank) is very likely registered with the Federal Reserve banking system (unless you, the grocery store, and the credit card company all happen to be using credit unions or state banks).

As such, NONE of the money involved actually _leaves_ the Fed banking system.

Even if you chose to pay for your gallon of milk in physical cash, the odds are quite high that the money _still_ ends up at a bank connected to the Federal Reserve banking system, albeit at a slower pace (when the grocery store deposits the physical cash in its business account).

Let's keep going with your day.

Now let's say that during your drive home from the store you hear that stocks are at new record highs on the radio. You decide you'd like to "cash out" some of the profits from your stock portfolio, so you call you broker and tell him or her to sell some shares.

Again...

    • The gas station where you purchased the fuel your
car is burning to drive home uses the Federal Reserve
payment system.

    • The radio station broadcasting the news about the
stock market uses the Federal Reserve payment system.

    • The cell phone company you are using for service
to call your broker uses the Federal Reserve payment
system.

    • The bank account into which you transfer your profits
from your brokerage account uses the Federal Reserve
payment system.

    • The payment system through which your broker col-
lects his or her commission fee for processing the sale of
your stocks uses the Federal Reserve payment system.

Moreover, it is HIGHLY likely that all of the bank accounts used
by the various businesses/ individuals listed above are part of the
Federal Reserve banking system as well.

Starting to see a trend here?

Put simply, on a day-to-day basis, trillions of dollars in wealth
moves around the US financial system via the Federal Reserve
payment system. And, wherever the money stops (a bank account) it's HIGHLY likely the account is with a firm that is part
of the Federal Reserve banking system.

I realize this can be difficult to wrap your head around. After all,
we're talking about a national payment and storage system that is
interconnected in a highly complicated manner. So, let me give
you a metaphor.

Imagine that money is like a car, the Fed payment system is like
the US roadway system, and the Fed Banking system is like pub-

lic parking locations throughout the United States.

Just as you can park your car in your own private garage, money might be "parked" in a bank or financial institution that isn't formally part of the Federal Reserve banking system.

However, if you want to "move" your money around the US financial system, with very few exceptions, you're going to use the Fed's payment system, just as your car will use the US roadway systems to get to your chosen destination when you're driving.

However, there is one key difference between my car metaphor and the reality of how money moves in the US financial system...

If people decide to start parking their cars at home instead of driving, the US roadways would continue to operate just fine.

In contrast, because of the structure of the US financial system, if enough of people decide to start "parking" their wealth in the form of cash (selling stocks or bonds to do so), it can cause a **financial crash.**

And, if they chose to move their money into actual *physical* cash, the whole system implodes.

No, I'm not being dramatic here.

Too Much Money Moving to Cash= Crashes or Systemic Risk

Few people know it, but the 2008 stock market crash of September to early November was in fact triggered by investors in a particular type of investment vehicle hitting "sell" and moving to actual cash.

The particular investment vehicle in this instance was called a Money Market Fund.

If you're unfamiliar with this term, this is a type of investment fund that takes investors' cash and invests it into short-term, highly liquid debt and credit securities.

The whole purpose of this investment vehicle is to offer investors a return on their cash in an extremely liquid investment vehicle (meaning investors can pull their money at any time).

It all sounds great in theory (getting your cash to pay out a return). But during the fall of 2008, investors panicked and started pulling their money out of these funds.

And not just a little…

During a four-week period from September to October 2008, Money Market Funds were hit with **$500 billion in withdrawals**. This represented close to 25% of all "money" kept in Money Market Funds at the time.

This was a "stampede for the exit." And as I noted before, in our current system, the "exit" is cash. And it was *THIS,* not the bankruptcy of Lehman Brothers, that triggered the stock market crash of 30%+ in the autumn of 2008.

Take a look at Chart 60 and you will see that stocks were already cratering well before Lehman Brothers failed on September 15, 2008. This was triggered by the collapse of the Money Market Fund industry.

Chart 60: S&P 500 Index Performance During Money Market Fund Panic (2008).

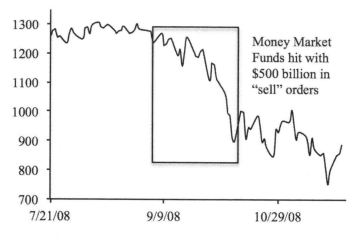

Note: Data adapted from Investing.com (2017)[18]

Again, financial crashes are triggered by large numbers of investors hitting "SELL" on asset classes and moving into cash.

As bad as that is, it's nothing compared to what would happen if investors chose to "cash out" their money from the financial markets and **then demanded their money in the form of physical cash.**

This would literally collapse the US banking system.

Again, I'm not being dramatic here. Technically speaking, the cash you keep in a bank account is a *liability* for the bank. Indeed, it is actually categorized as such on the bank's balance sheet, since the bank is "liable" for the funds if you ask for them back.

If you don't believe me, here's a screenshot from JP Morgan's actual 2016 financial statement:

Chart 61: JP Morgan Balance Sheet (2016).

Selected Consolidated balance sheets data

December 31, (in millions)	2016
Liabilities	
Deposits	$ 1,375,179
Federal funds purchased and securities loaned or sold under repurchase agreements	165,666
Commercial paper	11,738
Other borrowed funds	22,705
Trading liabilities:	
Debt and equity instruments	87,428
Derivative payables	49,231
Accounts payable and other liabilities	190,543
Beneficial interests issued by consolidated variable interest entities ("VIEs")	39,047
Long-term debt	295,245
Total liabilities	2,236,782
Stockholders' equity	254,190
Total liabilities and stockholders' equity	$ 2,490,972

Note: Retrieved from Securities and Exchange Commission (2017)[24]

Remember as I outlined earlier, there is $13.5 trillion in cash sitting in accounts in the United States. Meanwhile there is only $1.5 in physical cash in existence.

Put another way, the banks **don't have** trillions in physical dollar bills lying around in vaults to meet redemptions if people start demanding their money in actual physical cash.

For one thing, the money doesn't exist. And for another thing, storing even just $1 trillion would take up a space the size of a football field, even if the money were stored in $100 bills on warehouse-style pallets that were double stacked (meaning one pallet stacked on top of another).

In this context, if even 1% or 2% of the assets that make up the "wealth" in the US financial system (stocks, bonds, etc.) was "sold" and then investors asked their banks to withdraw the money to actual **physical cash**, the banking system would very quickly collapse.

Game. Over.

Which is why, the Fed will officially declare a War on Cash in the coming months, particularly when the Everything Bubble bursts.

This war will feature three strategies:

1) Negative Interest Rate Policy or NIRP.
2) Cash bans on large bill denominations ($100 or higher).
3) Carry taxes on smaller physical bill denominations ($1, $5, $10, and $20s).

Let's dive in.

NIRP: It's Not Just About Bonds, It's About Cash Too

We've already assessed how the Fed will use Negative Interest Rate Policy (NIRP) to drag down yields on short-term Treasuries.

However, there's a second component to NIRP, namely, that of making cash "painful" to hold.

I realize this might sound like conspiracy theory. But the reality is that in some ways this is just an extension of Fed monetary policy over the last 100+ years.

As Chart 62 shows, by depreciating the purchasing power of the US Dollar virtually non-stop, the Fed has made cash a losing asset class... something "painful" to own.

Chart 62. Purchasing Power of the US Dollar (1913-2016).

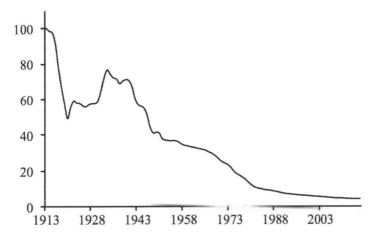

Note: Data adapted from Federal Reserve Bank of St. Louis (2017)[1]

Put simply, over the last 100+ years, those who have stockpiled cash have had to choose between sitting on their cash and watching as Fed policy erodes the purchasing power of their money OR moving their cash into other, potentially higher returning asset classes in an attempt to maintain their wealth.

In this sense, NIRP is just a hyper-aggressive version of this Fed policy in that it makes sitting on cash not just painful, but *REALLY* painful (you're losing money through loss of purchasing power AND being charged a negative interest rate).

Now, as I noted in the last chapter, the Fed will only be able to implement NIRP in the context of the crisis triggered by the bursting of the Everything Bubble; the American public wouldn't stand for it otherwise.

In *that* context, NIRP will be used as a reflationary tool in that it will:

1) Raise the "pain threshold" at which investors who own collapsing assets finally panic and move into cash.

2) Make sitting on cash so painful that those who are doing so already will eventually be forced to move into risk asset classes, thereby helping to reflate the financial system.

Regarding #1, as we noted earlier in this chapter, financial crashes are triggered by a large numbers of investors hitting "sell" on any given asset class. And in our current financial system hitting "sell" means selling an asset and *buying* cash.

So, let's consider how NIRP changes a hypothetical stockowner's thinking during a situation in which stocks have just fallen 10% and he or she is getting a bit nervous (see Chart 63).

Chart 63. How NIRP Changes Investment Outcomes and Thinking.

	Stay in Stocks	Sell Stocks and Move To Cash
Without NIRP	"I've just lost 10%, but stocks might bounce."	"I don't lose anything more and will earn a little on interest"
With NIRP	"I've just lost 10%, but stocks might bounce."	"I will *definitely* LOSE more money due to NIRP."

Put simply, NIRP shifts cash from a neutral asset (albeit one that loses purchasing power in the long-term) to a *negative* asset in the short-term. As such, the Fed hopes to use it as a policy tool with the goal being that when the Everything Bubble bursts, investors will be much more willing to maintain positions in various asset classes rather than panic and dump everything and move into cash.

The flip side of this is that the Fed also hopes that NIRP will force those who are already *in cash* to move into risk assets such as stocks and bonds, thereby helping to reflate the financial system.

Remember from earlier in this chapter, there is over $13 trillion in cash sitting in various accounts (Checking, Money Market, Certificates of Deposit, etc.) in the US financial system.

The Fed views this capital as "cash on the sidelines." And, when the Everything Bubble bursts, NIRP is the tool the Fed will use to drive this capital into the financial markets.

I realize this sounds like conspiracy theory, but the reality is that the Fed has already done precisely this, albeit less aggressively, for seven years via its Zero Interest Rate Policy (ZIRP) from 2008 to 2015.

With rates held at ZERO for seven years, the Fed created an environment in which anyone sitting on cash was earning effectively *nothing*. Moreover, because ZIRP and QE resulted in bond yields falling to record lows, anyone who was expecting to live off interest income via bonds was similarly out of luck.

Let's put this into dollar terms.

How ZIRP Was Used to "Punish" Cash Holders

From 1984 until 2007 (before the Fed implemented ZIRP), the average rate on a 12-month Certificate of Deposit (CD) was 5.2%. Over the same time period, the average yield on the 10-Year Treasury Note was 6.73%.

As a result of ZIRP, from 2008 until 2015 when the Fed raised rates for the first time since the 2008 crisis, the average rate on a 12-month CD fell to just 0.9% while the average yield on the 10-Year Treasury Note fell to just 2.75%.

Using this data, Chart 64 compares the average annual returns for a would-be retiree with $1 million invested in either a 12-month CD or the 10-Year Treasury Note under normal interest rate policy versus those generated by the same investments when ZIRP is in place.

It's not pretty.

Chart 64. How ZIRP Changed Investment Outcomes.

	$1 million in CD	$1 million in 10-Year Treasury
Average Annual Income 1984-2007	$52,008.33	$67,287.50
Average Annual Income 2008-2015	$9,638	$27,500.00
Difference	$42,370.83	$39,787.50

Note: Data adapted from Bankrate.com and Federal Reserve Bank of St. Louis (2017)[25,4]

As you can see, ZIRP was a form of punishment for anyone sitting on cash or Treasury bonds in that it drastically reduced their expected interest income. And because this punishment lasted **seven years,** eventually many Americans were forced to move their capital into riskier assets such as stocks or into longer-dated US Treasury Bonds (the 20-Year and 30-Year Treasury denominations typically yield more) to seek a higher return on their capital.

So in this sense, NIRP will simply be an even more extreme form of interest rate "punishment" by the Fed: a monetary tool the Fed uses to force those sitting on cash to eventually move into stocks and bonds, thereby helping to reflate the collapsing Everything Bubble in the process.

As such, NIRP will be one of the Fed's primary tools in its "War on Cash."

However, as I noted previously, NIRP only works if you cannot move your capital into physical cash.

After all, a good home safe costs only $400-$500. So, why would anyone with savings over $10,000 be willing to put up with NIRP of -3% or even -5%, when he or she can simply move into physical cash and avoid the annual fees entirely?

Which is why when the Fed moves to implement NIRP, it will

also be pushing for an actual ban on physical cash.

Based on policies already being used elsewhere in the world, as well as proposals that financial regulators have been itching to put into practice, I believe this cash ban will take two forms:

1) An actual ban on physical cash, particularly for large bill denominations ($100 bills or greater).

2) A "carry tax" on smaller physical bill denominations ($1, $5, $10, and $20s).

If this sounds completely insane to you, consider that it's simply a virtual repeat of what the United States did with physical *gold* back in the 1930s.

The US Has Already Banned Physical Money Once Before

The US has already banned physical money once before when the Franklin Delano Roosevelt banned the ownership of physical gold in 1933. The only reason we don't think of this as a ban on "money" per se, is that today most Americans see the US dollar as "money," while gold is thought to be "an investment."

However, back in 1933, when the US Federal Reserve was only 20 years old, and the United States was still on the Gold Standard, gold was still very much considered "money." So, when the Roosevelt administration banned the ownership of gold, it was effectively banning physical cash in its most popular form.

In this context, it's worth doing a brief review of how that "money ban" went. You'll note that there are a number of striking similarities between the issues the US financial system was facing then and those it faces now.

As I outlined in Chapter 1, *How Debt Became Money*, during the early 1930s, the United States experienced a systemic banking crisis brought about by the bursting of a massive debt bubble (sounds familiar?).

Because the US dollar was still linked to gold at that time, gold was considered "money." Indeed, for most Americans, it was widely thought to be **sound money** since the US dollar had already lost 20% of its purchasing power due to Fed monetary policy in the preceding 20 years.

So, when the debt bubble of the 1920s burst, plunging the United States into a banking crisis, Americans began pulling their money out of the banks in the form of **physical gold.**

As is the case with physical cash today, this represented a massive problem for the Federal Reserve banking system because:

1) It meant money was leaving the banking system (no longer subject to Fed policy).

2) Banks had a limited supply of physical gold. So when Americans opted to remove their savings in gold, the banks' financial conditions *worsened*, leading to more bank failures.

To deal with this, then-President Franklin Delano Roosevelt did the following:

1) Made it illegal for Americans to own gold.

2) Confiscated physical gold, forcing Americans to own US dollars.

3) Devalued the US dollar by 70% against gold (the equivalent of a massive amount of money printing).

So again, there is indeed precedent for the US government to confiscate *physical* money from Americans.

And, when the Everything Bubble bursts and debt deflation grips the markets once again as it did back in the early 1930s, you can expect a near repeat of the above, only with "physical cash" substituting for "physical gold" (though gold will also probably be banned again for the same reason).

Here's how it will work.

The Coming Ban on Large Bills

Truth be told, globally a War on Cash is already underway, with many countries having banned the use of physical cash from key transactions.

In the last few years, France, Italy, Spain, and other European Union members have banned the use of physical cash for transactions over a certain amount (usually €1,000 or higher). India even went so far as to remove over 86% of all physical cash from its economy by banning the 500 rupee and 1,000 rupee notes: the two most common bills in circulation.

These countries are not unusual either.

Around the world, governments are drafting legislation to implement bans on physical cash for certain transactions in places as varied as Australia, Canada, New Zealand, and Mexico. And some countries (Norway, Denmark, and Sweden) are pushing to ban the use of physical cash altogether.

So in this sense, the United States is actually a little "behind the times" when it comes to the War on Cash. However, the Fed and other financial regulators will more than make up for this when the Everything Bubble bursts.

Indeed, numerous high level financial insiders have already begun calling for a ban on the $500 bill and other large denomination bills... and this is before the next crisis has even begun!

Among those publicly calling for cash bans on large bill denominations are:

- Larry Summers (former Secretary of the Treasury to President Bill Clinton)
- Professor Ken Rogoff (former Chief Economist to the International Monetary Fund or IMF)
- Narayana Kocherlakota (former Minneapolis Fed President)
- Joseph Gagnon (former Associate Director for the Federal Reserve Board)

This is a veritable who's who of financial elite: individuals with close ties to the highest levels of the US Treasury, the Federal Reserve, and the International Monetary Fund.

The fact that these individuals are already calling for a ban on large bills tells us that this topic is being discussed at the highest levels within the US financial system.

This is why I believe that when the Everything Bubble bursts, and the US financial system experiences debt deflation again, we'll be seeing calls for an outright cash ban on large bill denominations.

This will be sold to the public as an attempt to stop tax evasion, money laundering, or some other illicit activity. However, as we've already outlined, the real reason the Fed will want to ban large cash denominations will be to make it more difficult to move large quantities of capital into physical money.

Consider that $100,000 stacked in $100 bills is roughly only four inches high: a very manageable pile to move and store. Indeed, even $1 million in $100 bills is still small enough that it can be easily stored in a small home safe.

However, try moving and storing this much money when it's denominated in small bills ($10s or $20s) and the pile gets significantly larger.

At that point:

1) The money is much more conspicuous to take out of a bank, thereby making you a target for robbery.

2) The money is much more difficult to keep track of (if some goes missing it's harder to tell… not to mention counting it takes much longer).

3) The money is much more difficult to store privately as it takes up more space.

In this sense, banning larger bill denominations makes getting your money out of the Federal Reserve banking system much more difficult. Those who would opt to do so to avoid NIRP might be inclined to think twice, especially if they're going to be taking out a significant amount of money (say $50,000 or higher).

Now I wish I could say that banning large bills will be the End Game for the Fed's coming War on Cash. Unfortunately, I believe the Fed will have another policy up its sleeve for anyone who is still willing to go through the hassle of moving their savings out of the banking system in smaller bill denominations.

I'm talking about a carry tax.

The Carry Tax: Cash Loses Value Over Time

Right now, you're probably asking, *"What's a carry tax?"*

A carry tax is a tax the Government imposes on those who "carry" around physical cash.

This idea has been floating around Central Banking circles for decades. Indeed, the Fed actually published a research paper advocating for this policy back in 2000 (more on this shortly).

The only reason no one has actually attempted to implement this strategy is that politically it's so toxic that it would require a massive crisis and consequent panic for this legislation to be approved.

A massive crisis like… the bursting of the Everything Bubble.

Hard to believe, how would it even work?

The way it would work is that when you go to take your money out of the bank in physical form, the bills would be stamped or scanned in such a way as to record the date and time at which the withdrawal took place.

Then, whenever the bill is finally deposited back into a bank again, the receiving bank would use this information to deduct a certain percentage of the bill's value as a "tax" for holding it, much as parking garages use tickets to determine what to charge you for parking your car a certain amount of time.

For instance, if the rate was 5% per month and you withdrew a $20 bill that you carried around for two months before depositing back in the bank, the receiving bank would only register the deposit as being worth $18.05 ($20 X 0.95 = $19 for the first month, and then $19 X 0.95 = $18.05 for the second month).

Ok, you're definitely insane.

Really? Because the Fed itself proposed this **exact policy in a research paper:**

*To supplement the carry tax on electronic reserves, **a carry tax could be imposed on currency by imbedding a magnetic strip in each bill**. The magnetic strip could visibly record when a bill was last withdrawn from the banking system. **A carry tax could be deducted from each bill upon deposit according got how long the bill was in circulation since last withdrawn and how much carry tax was "past due."** Likewise, a carry tax could be assessed on currency held as vault cash in banks.*
[emphasis added]:

~Goodfriend, M. (2000, August) Overcoming The Zero Bound on Interest Rate Policy.
Retrieved from www.richmondfed.org/publications/research/working_papers/2000/wp_00-3

Lest anyone might think the goal here was related to raising taxes or something else, the author states point blank that this is about STOPPING people from SITTING ON CASH:

> **"The carry tax would serve as a powerful deterrent to hoarding currency.** *Currency that was hoarded and "past due" would only be accepted at a discount sufficient to cover the arrears"*

Again, this is a research paper, published by **the Federal Reserve itself** and written by an economist who has since gone on to be a visiting scholar for THREE Central Banks as well as the International Monetary Fund.

How's that for nuts?

Truth be told, this policy isn't even that crazy. Technically speaking, the Fed has been engaging in a War on Cash via the "stealth" tax of currency devaluation since it was first created in 1913.

Remember Chart 65?

Chart 65. Purchasing Power of the US Dollar (1913-2016).

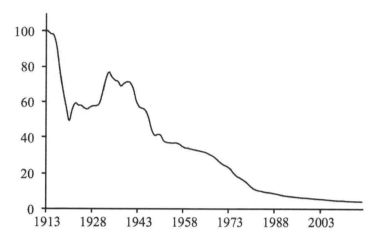

Note: Data adapted from Federal Reserve Bank of St. Louis (2017)[1]

The Fed's devaluation of the US dollar and its purchasing power has acted as a stealth tax on cash since 1913. Put another way, if you kept your capital in cash for any significant period of time over the last 100 years, you've lost "money" practically every year in the sense that your cash is losing its purchasing power.

How is directly taxing physical cash outright any different?

The United States populace has already put up with this for over 100 years. So, when the Everything Bubble bursts and the Fed and other financial regulators begin openly declaring a War on Cash via NIRP, cash bans, and carry taxes, they will simply be taking a pre-existing policy (the gradual punishment of those who own cash) to its most extreme.

Again, the goal here is to make sitting on cash so "painful" that it will force Americans to move their capital into risk assets (particularly stocks and bonds) where it (the capital) will help reflate the collapsing financial system.

I realize this sounds crazy, but once again, I will remind you that the notions of the Fed running seven years of ZIRP and spending $3.5 trillion in QE would have sounded crazy before 2008.

My point is that when major crises hit, the Fed is able to implement truly extraordinary policies with little political fall-out. Given what is at stake, when the Everything Bubble bursts, I have little doubt the Fed will be doing everything it can to stop capital from fleeing the financial system.

This will inevitably lead the Fed to NIRP, cash bans, and carry taxes. Unfortunately, this won't be the end of the punishment either.

As we've already laid out in the preceding chapters, the Everything Bubble is so massive in scope that even NIRP, nuclear levels of QE, and cash bans (both literal and via carry taxes) won't be able to stop the inevitable debt deflation, particularly when it comes to banks that are over-exposed to garbage debt (bad loans they've made based on false risk assumptions).

For this reason, when the Everything Bubble bursts, those who choose to ignore the "pain" of NIRP and decide to sit on their cash in a bank account will face yet another risk: a bail-in, or the process through which a percentage of cash deposits are raided or converted into stock in the bank.

These bail-ins will not be exclusive to indebted banks either. Anyone sitting on significant pools of capital (an amount greater than the FDIC-insured limit of $250,000 or its equivalent in cash savings) will eventually be called on to bail-in the financial system via a wealth tax.

This will mean experiencing a "haircut" (meaning you lose a percentage of your capital completely) in order to improve the government's poor fiscal situation.

Whether this will be a one-time deal or simply the first in a series of wealth taxation schemes remains to be seen.

But in simple terms…

Prepare to be taxed.

CHAPTER 9:
BAIL-INS AND WEALTH TAXES

Thus far, we've outlined two components of the Fed's policy response for when the Everything Bubble bursts.

They are:

1) To prop up the US debt markets, particularly US sovereign debt or Treasuries, via NIRP and nuclear levels of QE.

2) To stop capital from fleeing the financial system via cash bans and carry taxes.

In pictorial form, the Fed's hope with these policies is that it will stop both the solid and the dotted lines in Chart 66 from falling.

Chart 66. Total US Debt Securities and Cash/Cash Equivalents, Trillions US Dollars (1981-2016).

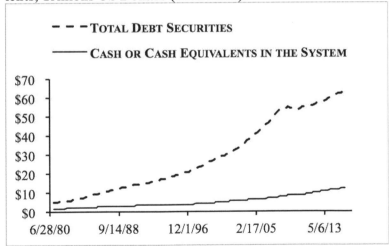

Note: Data adapted from Federal Reserve Bank of St. Louis (2017)[3,26]

If the solid line falls, the US financial system experiences debt deflation similar to what triggered the 2008 financial crisis. NIRP and nuclear levels of QE are meant to stop this.

If the dotted line falls, the US experiences a banking crisis similar to that of the 1930s. Cash bans and carry taxes are meant to stop this.

As extreme as these policies are, they likely won't prove sufficient to stopping the Everything Bubble from collapsing. It's simply too large! As a result of this, the Fed will eventually reach the End Game for central bank policy.

Let me explain.

When the Fed created a bubble in US Treasuries in the aftermath of the housing crash, it altered the risk landscape for the ENTIRE debt market. Put another way, any entity (bank, corporation, state government, or even individual consumers) that has borrowed money aggressively since 2009 has done so based on a FALSE risk profile courtesy of the Fed's interventions.

As a result of this, the Everything Bubble is in fact one gigantic debt bubble comprised of numerous smaller, individual debt bubbles… bubbles in corporate debt, municipal debt, consumer debt, commercial debt, etc.

As such, **the ENTIRE $60 trillion in debt securities floating around the US financial system is vulnerable to debt deflation when the Everything Bubble bursts.**

So, while the Fed *might* be able to prop up the Treasury market via QE programs, there is simply NO WAY it can prop up everything. And, at some point, some segment of the debt markets will begin to experience a wave of defaults. When this happens, those firms with significant exposure to that area of the debt markets will begin to face solvency issues.

Firms that are smaller or deemed less "systemically important" to the banking system will be allowed to fail or will be swallowed up by larger firms, much like what happened to Bear Stearns in 2008 when its exposure to subprime mortgage debt resulted in it being acquired by JP Morgan in a "shotgun wedding."

However, at some point a larger systemically important firm will get into trouble. And that's when the threat of contagion will become real (think mid-2008 when the mortgage giants Fannie and Freddie began to implode and the US financial system teetered on the verge of collapse).

The Fed will then face the End Game for monetary policy, particularly QE. It will have to choose, either it:

1) Attempts to monetize **everything** (starts buying any and all deflating debt assets).
2) Seeks other sources of capital to prop up failing institutions/ firms.

Regarding #1, the Fed *might* be able to get away with buying *some* debt securities other than Treasuries, provided it had political cover to do so. For instance, the Fed was able to buy mortgage-backed debt securities via QE 1 and QE 3 because those policies were supposed to benefit the housing market/ homeowners.

However, given how politically unsavory bailouts have become, it's unlikely the Fed would be able to get away with buying extensive debt securities for long. And, the fact is that with some $60 trillion in debt securities outstanding, even a massive, non-Treasury related QE program wouldn't accomplish much.

In this context, when debt deflation begins to appear in debt markets *outside* of Treasuries, the Fed and other regulators will be forced to take option #2: **seeking other sources of capital to prop up failing institutions/ firms.**

This will ultimately lead to Bail-Ins and Wealth Taxes.

If these terms are unfamiliar to you, you can think of both of them as "capital grabs," through which regulators simply *TAKE* money from those who are sitting on it in order to prop up failing/ defaulting institutions.

How is this different from outright theft?

It's not. However, if presented with a choice between A) losing a percentage of their money so their bank stays in business or B) losing all of their money and the bank fails, **most people will opt for option A.**

Moreover, these policies won't be promoted in advance; by the time regulators are discussing a bail-in for a given bank, that bank will already be closed via a "holiday." So you can forget about protesting in advance or trying to get your money out.

I realize all of this might be hard to swallow. After all, we're taught from an early age that "money in the bank" is safe. Indeed, the entire US banking system functions based on this sense of confidence. So the notion that a bank might simply *take* your funds seems outrageous.

However, the unfortunate reality is this scheme has already been utilized **multiple times**. And, not in some 3rd world dictatorship, but in Europe where as much as 40% of deposits above a certain threshold were seized by regulators to prop up failing financial institutions.

The country I'm talking about is Cyprus. And the banks involved were Laiki and the Bank of Cyprus, the two largest, most systemically important banks in the country.

Buckle up...what follows is both horrifying and morally reprehensible. But, unfortunately it has become the template for how regulators and the political classes will be dealing with failing, systemically important banks and institutions going forward.

Indeed, already Canada, New Zealand, the United Kingdom, Germany, and even the United States have developed legislation that would permit similar Bail-In schemes to be used.

The following is a technical breakdown of the European Union (EU) debt crisis that ultimately culminated in Cyprus' bank Bail-Ins. If you are not interested in these details and simply want to continue on to the how Bail-Ins will be introduced in the United States in the future, skip ahead to the section titled, *Bail-Ins: Coming to a Bank Near You.*

Europe: Bankrupt Banks Buying Bankrupt Nations' Debts

Since 2010, Europe's banking system has been in a state of near perpetual crisis.

This topic only grabs headlines when a major development hits like a bank collapsing, but the reality is Europe's banking system has been teetering on the brink of insolvency for years now.

The reasons for this are as follows.

1) EU nations are massively indebted due to decades of rampant social spending programs.
2) EU banks are overleveraged due to having made far too many loans during Europe's own housing bubble (2002-2007).
3) EU banks ALSO own EU member states' bonds (so you've got bankrupt banks, owning bankrupt nations' debts).

Regarding #1, the EU as a whole is largely socialist.

This means that a large portion of EU member-state economies are tied to public employment. Indeed, Germany is often held up as a free-market economy, but even that country derives nearly one third of its employment from the government (compared to 16% for the United States).

Socialist nations, by their very nature, have large social spending/ welfare programs. However, in Europe's case, these programs have become truly massive due to the fact that most of the region has aging populations that require higher healthcare expenditures and retirement benefits.

Moreover, no one wants to stop. Since usually 30% or more of voters are employed by or have family members employed by the government, Europeans keep voting for politicians who want to grow the government and increase social spending.

As is the case for the United States, all of Europe's social spending programs are financed by taxes. And, if taxes cannot cover an EU member's entitlement spending, **the country turns to the debt markets for funding.**

The reason the EU went into an actual debt crisis is because many member states were already massively indebted when they joined the union (they had lied about their true debt obligations in order to join).

So right off the bat, the EU was headed for financial failure since it was simply linking together a group of highly indebted nations.

However, what *really* made this situation boil over was the fact that when new countries joined the EU, the interest rate at which they could issue debt usually dropped in a big way as they were now backed by the full faith and credit of the EU (18+ countries) instead of their own standalone creditworthiness.

I realize this is getting a bit dense. So imagine that you know 18 different people who all have significant credit card debt and low-to-terrible credit scores.

Now, imagine that these 18 people decided to pool ALL of their finances together into one bank account.

Now, imagine that by joining together, these 18 people all get access to a new credit card policy with an unlimited balance and an ultra low interest rate.

That's the EU in a nutshell.

Which brings us to item #2 in the list above (EU banks and their leverage issues).

Like the United States, the EU also had a massive housing bubble leading up to 2007. And, because much of the EU banking system was less regulated than that of the United States, EU banks went on absolutely insane lending sprees, lending money to anyone and anything looking to buy or develop property from 2002 to 2007.

As a result of this, going into the 2008 Financial Crisis, EU banks had grown to sizes that were systemically dangerous. You can see this in Chart 67.

Chart 67. Bank Assets to Gross Domestic Product Ratios for Deposit Banks By Country (2008).

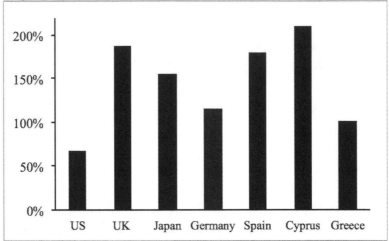

Note: Data adapted from Federal Reserve Bank of St. Louis (2017)[27]

Looking at Chart 67 you might be thinking, *"wait a minute, both the United Kingdom and Japan had bank asset to GDP ratios nearly as high as Cyprus... why weren't they in serious trouble?"*

The United Kingdom and Japan both have their own currencies that can be printed via their respective Central Banks. In contrast, individual EU nations **cannot** print the Euro, only the European Central Bank (ECB) can. So, if individual EU nations get into trouble, they have to turn to the ECB for help (more on this shortly).

Of the EU nations, Cyprus banks were the most systemically dangerous with a total bank asset to GDP ratio of 213%. To give you an idea of how insane this is, consider that the US banking system would need to have assets of over $31 TRILLION to match this ratio (we're talking about strictly "plain vanilla" assets such as commcial loans here, not Over the Counter derivatives).

In this context (an overleveraged banking system with broad exposure to bankrupt EU nations' sovereign debts), when the EU first entered a debt crisis in 2009, the flaws in the system quickly became evident.

The first round of the Crisis involved the infamous PIIGS countries (Portugal, Ireland, Italy, Greece and Spain) experiencing brief bouts of sovereign debt deflation. Because these nations also used the Euro as their currency, and only the ECB could print the Euro, the EU was forced to deal with these situations via a combination of bailouts and market rigs.

Without going into too much detail, these deals usually involved the individual countries receiving a special loan package from the EU, ECB and the International Monetary Fund (IMF), in exchange for the promise of entitlement spending cuts.

These policies work for a time: from 2010-2012, the ECB, EU and IMF bailed out Greece (twice), Hungary, Ireland, Latvia, Portugal, Romania, and Spain.

However, by the time the end of 2012 rolled around, the European voting public, particularly citizens in those nations that had yet to experience systemic debt problems (France and Germany,) were becoming increasingly fed up with funding all of these bailouts.

As a result of this, when Cyprus' banking system started to implode due to its overexposure to Greek sovereign debt in 2012, the EU opted for a new program...

The bank Bail-_IN_.

The Cyprus Bail-In: A New Template For Troubled Banks

How's a bail-in different from a bailout?

A bailout means the funds being used are from external sources (another firm, a central bank, a country, etc.). In contrast, a bail-*in* means the funds are coming from the troubled entity itself.

Wait a minute… how can a firm that is failing bail itself out?

It can't and it doesn't. Technically, the people keeping deposits/capital at the firm are the ones funding the deal.

Remember from Chapter 8, *The War on Cash*, that the funds you store in a bank are considered liabilities by the bank. So, when we talk about bail-ins, what we're technically talking about is the bank TAKING *your* money and using it to deal with its solvency issues.

We're not talking about a loan either. We're talking about either:

1) Your funds are simply confiscated so the bank owns them outright (you never get them back).

2) Your funds are converted into equity in the bank at some arbitrary price and you're not permitted to sell your shares for months (during which time the shares could drop, wiping out your capital).

In the case of Cyprus in 2013, regulators **froze** bank accounts at the two largest banks (the Bank of Cyprus and Laiki) and then **seized a certain percentage of all deposits** above €100,000 in order to bail-in the banks.

Here's the timeline for how it played out:

> • 2011-early 2012: Cyprus banks with broad exposure to Greek sovereign debt take a massive hit during the first Greek bailout. Over the next six months the Cyprus banking system begins lurching towards a crisis.

- June 25, 2012: Cyprus formally requests a bailout from the EU.

- November 24, 2012: Cyprus announces it has reached an agreement with the EU regarding a bailout (at that time Cyprus banks were estimated to need €17.5 billion in capital: an amount roughly the size of Cyprus's economy).

- Saturday, March 16, 2013: Cyprus suddenly announces that it won't be seeking a bailout but will instead employ a bail-in, confiscating 6.75% of accounts under €100,000 and 9.9% of accounts larger than €100,000. **That same day a bank holiday is announced**.

At that point Cyprus banks were closed and Cyprus citizens couldn't get their money out except for small daily withdrawals (usually €100-€400) from ATMs.

Let's keep going…

- Sunday, March 17, 2013: Cyprus' parliament postpones its vote on the proposed bail-in.

- Monday, March 18, 2013: the Cyprus bank holiday is extended until Thursday, March 21, 2013.

- Tuesday, March 19, 2013: Cyprus' parliament rejects the bail-in bill.

- Wednesday, March 20, 2013: the Cyprus bank holiday is extended until Tuesday, March 26, 2013.

- Monday, March 25, 2013: Cyprus' parliament agrees on a bail-in deal. Deposits over €100,000 at Laiki are wiped out forever. In contrast, roughly 50% of all deposits over €100,000 at the Bank of Cyprus are converted into the bank's stock (the shares of which later collapsed, wiping out the funds).

Put simply, if you had more than €100,000 at either bank, you either lost ALL of the money above this threshold immediately, or half of your money above this threshold was converted into bank stock… which then promptly collapsed, wiping you out.

As horrifying as this is, the most important item I want you to focus on is the *pacing* of these events.

Cyprus formally requested a bailout from the EU in **June 2012**. The bailout talks took a total of nine months, during which time it *appeared* as if a bailout would occur.

Then, in the span of a single week, the talks fell apart, and the whole banking system came unhinged.

One week.

The process was not gradual. It was sudden and it was total: once it began in earnest, the banks were closed and Cypriots couldn't get their money out (more on this in a moment).

The public was livid as you can imagine. However, the political class sold this wealth confiscation scheme as being about… you guessed it, cracking down on illicit activities. In this particular case, the claim was that most of the large bank accounts at the two banks belonged to tax-evading Russian mobsters.

The reality is that the Russian mobster story was just a cover for outright theft. Behind the scenes, "those in the know" alerted their families and friends of what was coming, leading to 132 government-connected companies getting their money (some $916 million in capital) out ahead of time.

The general public, in contrast, was screwed.

By the time the banking holiday was over, Cypriots had lost hundreds of thousands of Euros' in wealth. The riots, protests, and outrage accomplished nothing. The money was gone.

Most importantly as far as the political class was concerned...
the whole scheme played out with few casualties from a career
perspective (only the Finance Minister resigned). And, those
politicians who remained in office (almost all of them) touted
the bail-ins as a success because they (the bail-ins) didn't use
taxpayer funds.

Put simply, the Cyprus bail-ins showed the world's political
classes that A) you can simply STEAL people's savings and use
them to prop up failing banks and B) doing this results in virtually no one in the political sphere losing his or her job.

Governments around the world took note... and began hashing
out similar strategies for dealing with future banking crises.
Canada, New Zealand, the United Kingdom, and even Germany,
developed legislation that would permit similar bail-in schemes
to be used should their respective banks ever get into trouble.

And if you think that regulators in the United States haven't
implemented something similar, you've got another surprise
coming.

Bail-Ins: Coming to a Bank Near You

As I outlined in Chapter 8, *The War on Cash*, there is roughly
$13.5 trillion in "cash" sitting in various bank accounts in the
United States.

Now, technically, the Federal Deposit Insurance Corporation
(FDIC) is meant to voer any account with a balance below
$250,000. So, provided that this $13.5 trillion in cash is all stored
in accounts with balances of $250,000 or less, it's safe.

Not so fast...

It's a little known fact that, the FDIC, the organization in charge of insuring those $13.5 TRILLION in deposits, has less than $100 billion in capital available to do this.

This stands at less than 1% of the deposits in the US financial system. Heck, it isn't even enough to cover the deposits at a single large bank if any of them failed (JP Morgan alone has over $1.3 trillion in deposits).

Which is why, in the aftermath of the Financial Crisis of 2008, the FDIC began exploring alternative means of propping up what it calls Systemically Important Financial Entities, or SIFIs.

The template it developed looks a lot like the bail-in strategy used in Cyprus. And don't even bother hoping that this proposal was turned down by Congress: Title II of the Dodd-Frank Wall Street "reform" bill of 2010 has already given the FDIC legal authority to intervene should a firm that it deems a SIFI starts to fail.

According to this legislation,when a SIFI begins to fail:

1) The FDIC would step in and take over the SIFI's business.
2) Culpable senior management at the SIFI would be "removed."
3) Losses would then be "apportioned to shareholders and unsecured creditors."

That last point is basically legal speak for *"people who own the SIFI's stock or unsecured debt would lose some, if not all, of their money."*

Here's how it would work…

The FDIC would first wipe out stockholders, or anyone who

owned stock in the SIFI. If the capital seized by doing this failed to be render the SIFI solvent, the FDIC would then start wiping out those who bought the SIFI's unsecured debt (any of its bonds that were not backstopped by some form of collateral).

The FDIC doesn't sugar coat the likely outcome of this:

> *In all likelihood, shareholders* [read: those owning stock] ***would lose all value*** *and unsecured creditors should thus expect that their claims would be **written down to reflect any losses that shareholders did not cover**.*
> [edits & emphasis added]
>
> *Resolving Globally Active, Systemically Important, Financial Institutions.* Federal Deposit Insurance Corporation and Bank of England, 2012, www.fdic.gov/about/srac/2012/gsifi.pdf
> Accessed 4 September 2017.

So basically, if you own stock in the firm, you lose everything. And if you own unsecured debt in the firm, unless the capital seized from stockholders can resolve the firm's solvency issues, you're losing money too.

But what about depositors... are their funds at risk as well?

The FDIC is explicit that the goal of its new program would be to get the SIFI solvent/ operational again. To do this, the FDIC would seek to reduce the SIFI's liabilities.

There are two ways the FDIC would do this. It could either:

1) Write down the value of these liabilities, meaning the FDIC simply says, *"this liability is no longer worth 100 cents on the dollar but is now worth a lower amount, (e.g. 50 cents on the dollar, 30 cents on the dollar, etc.)."*

219

2) Convert these liabilities into new equity or stock in the firm.

Regarding strategy #1, as I outlined in Chapter 8, *The War on Cash*, the deposits you keep in a bank are considered liabilities. So any capital you keep in a bank above the FDIC insured limit of $250,000 could simply be written down… meaning a percentage, if not all, of these funds would be **wiped out.**

Just like what happened in the Cyprus bank Laiki.

In contrast, strategy #2 means that any capital you keep in a bank above the FDIC insured limit of $250,000 is converted into equity in the bank. In this scenario, technically speaking this would mean that you would keep 100% of your funds over the $250,000 threshold, as they would simply be converted from cash into stock.

However, there is one small problem…

Stock prices change every minute that the market is open. And your capital has been converted into stock in a bank that the **entire world** knows is in big trouble (the FDIC's seizure and bail-in would undoubtedly have grabbed headlines throughout the media).

So, what do you think is going to happen to the bank's stock price once the company is actively traded on the markets again?

If you guessed, "it's going to collapse," you'd be correct.

Indeed, this is precisely what happened during the Bank of Cyprus' bail-in. In that particular case, roughly 50% of all uninsured deposits were to be converted into shares in the bank at a nominal value of €1.00 per share (ultimately only 37.5% of these deposits were used).

Whatever initial relief these depositors at the Bank of Cyprus felt at not losing their funds was promptly erased when shares in the bank collapsed to €0.20 on the open market.

Put another way, **these depositors lost 80% of their capital**.

So, even if the FDIC opts to convert deposits into stock in the SIFI, those funds are not safe by any means. Again, this all comes back to the fact that deposits are liabilities for banks. As such, the FDIC will want to reduce them along with all other liabilities as it moves to get the SIFI solvent again.

I realize all of the above sounds completely outrageous. Unfortunately, as I've already outlined, the above policies are not some nutty scheme published in an academic journal somewhere; **they've already been signed into law.**

Now anyone with a functioning brain would read the above and simply move to get his or her capital out of any bank that is deemed systemically important at the first sign of trouble.

However, just what precisely qualifies as a SIFI is confusing. One definition is any bank with over $50 billion in assets (there are 36 of them). Another definition is any firm that the Financial Stability Board deems a SIFI (it publishes a list every year).

However, the reality is that neither of those definitions is comprehensive. Let's say a bank with $30 billion in assets begins to collapse. Do you really think that somehow the FDIC won't deem it systemically important?

Moreover, as we've noted previously, there are over $170 trillion in derivatives floating around the US financial system, many of them completely unregulated. NO ONE knows just which firm is exposed to what and by how much. And, expecting the banks to accurately assess how much of this is "at risk" is like asking a drunk to honestly assess if he or she has a problem.

Put simply, the Dodd-Frank reform bill has opened the door to bail-ins being used to deal with any firm that the FDIC deems "systemically important." When the Everything Bubble bursts, that definition will very likely change to involve more banks than you'd guess.

Like I said at the beginning of this section, "bail-ins: coming to a bank near you." And for those pools of capital that *aren't* at risk of being used in a bail-in, the regulators and political classes have another scheme up their sleeves.

I'm talking about "Wealth Taxes."

Wealth Taxes and Cash Grabs

As I've explained throughout this chapter, when the Everything Bubble bursts, the Fed and financial regulators will be forced to seek other sources of capital to "plug" the various debt deflation "leaks" in the financial system.

The fact is, the Everything Bubble is simply too large to contain via interest rate policy and QE programs. And truth be told, I believe that even Bail-Ins won't prove adequate either.

After all, the regulators can't simply just sit on their hands waiting for a Systemically Important Financial Institution, or SIFI, to fail in order to get access to capital. Debt deflation will be appearing in all kinds of debt markets long before a major financial firm starts getting into serious trouble.

For this reason, I fully expect regulators to work with the political class to implement Wealth Taxes as a means of securing more capital.

What do I mean by "Wealth Taxes"?

I mean:

1) Taxes on luxury goods.
2) Confiscating unclaimed assets.
3) Implementing a one-off tax (say 10%) on **net wealth.**

I realize that this prediction, like many in this book, sounds like conspiracy theory. But the truth is, the United States has already used #1 and #2 before.

And, with wealth inequality having grown to historic records due to the Fed's creation of the Everything Bubble (bubbles inherently favor the wealthy who can borrow money using low interest rates to acquire more assets to profit from the bubble), it's only a small leap in logic to get to #3.

Let's dive in.

Regarding #1, the proposal here would be to tax any item that is considered a luxury good (something that is unnecessary). I'm talking about watches, artwork, private jets, and the like.

Put simply, if you own something really expensive that isn't required for your day-to-day life or the day-to-day operations of your business, the US government will want to tax it.

If you think I'm fooling around here, consider that the United States actually did exactly this back in 1991, charging a 10% "luxury surcharge tax" on everything from boats to aircraft, expensive furs, luxury jewelry, and other items valued above a certain price.

As is always the case, this scheme was sold as being about the greater good (in this case the rich were meant to help cover the deficit), but the reality was that it was just another cash grab.

Worst part of all?

The political class discovered that it worked. No one got kicked out of office for promoting or voting for this scheme. And, Congress managed to raise $8.9 billion of its $9 billion target. If you think Congress viewed this as a "failure," you don't understand how the government thinks about taxes.

Indeed, the only reason Congress bailed on the scheme was because people stopped buying expensive boats, watches and the like. So, Congress stopped taxing those goods. But it let the tax on luxury cars run **another 10 years.**

Put simply, a luxury tax has happened in the United States before. Truth be told, it wasn't that long ago. And, when the Everything Bubble bursts, it's likely to happen again particularly now that wealth inequality is at historic extremes.

Once again this will be passed off as an effort to cut down on wealth inequality, but the reality is that it's just another cash grab by authorities looking to shore up an insolvent financial system.

Which brings us to #2 in our list above: the confiscation of unclaimed assets.

Unclaimed Assets: If You Don't Use It, You Lose It

What's an "unclaimed asset"?

The term unclaimed asset is basically legal speak for "money that technically belongs to someone, but the person never claimed it, has forgotten about it, or doesn't even know it exists."

We're talking about apartment security deposits, money kept in safe deposit boxes at banks, certificates of deposit (CDs) that have come due, unclaimed life insurance payouts, payroll checks that haven't been cashed, unused gift certificates/ gift cards, and the like.

By some estimates, somewhere between $30 billion and $50 billion in wealth is sitting in unclaimed assets. So, we're not talking about loose change in between couch cushions here.

Now, technically, the firm or entity that is "holding" these assets (banks, state governments, etc.) is supposed to "attempt" to contact the rightful owner. However, what exactly connotes an "attempt" is vague at best (is sending one letter enough? sending two? sending an email?).

Moreover, unless the firm or entity has your most recent contact information, it's highly unlikely that you'll even receive the notification.

By law, after a certain period of time, authorities are permitted to seize unclaimed assets, auction off the items that are not in a liquid, cash state, and then use the proceeds to balance government budgets. This has been the case in the United States for years, but once the Everything Bubble bursts, I expect the pace at which unclaimed assets are seized and sold off will be going into overdrive.

Haven't visited your safe deposit box in a few years?

The bank can and, probably will, seize it, auction off its contents, and pass the cash along to your state's government.

Didn't claim you Certificate of Deposit when it came due?

Ditto.

Got a bunch of paychecks lying around that you never cashed?

Your state government has probably already cashed them for

you... well not *for you*, but *for the state,* so to speak.

You get the general idea.

In the simplest of terms, when it comes to capital that is just lying around, when the Everything Bubble bursts, the authorities' motto will be "use it or lose it." And if you haven't used it in a while, you'll likely lose it pretty quickly.

Which brings us to our final option, or #3 in our original list of coming cash grabs: a one-off tax on net wealth.

A Tax on Net Wealth (Assets+ Capital- Debt)

In this scenario, financial regulators would work with the US Treasury to impose a one-time tax on net wealth: NOT cash in the bank, but NET WEALTH... as in the net value of everything you own (assets + capital – debt = the amount being taxed).

Before you label me insane, let's first take a moment to review the maze of taxes every $1 in your bank account had to navigate before it became "your money."

If you receive income from working in the United States economy (as opposed to receiving a social entitlement or a welfare check), the business or entity that "pays" you first has to pay a whole slew of taxes before it even writes you a check.

These include: sales taxes on goods or services sold (true for most states), property taxes, excise taxes on use or consumption of various goods and services (fuel, transportation, communications), and finally payroll taxes on your actual paycheck.

But wait, we're just getting started.

This money is still technically not all yours. Once the business actually hands you your paycheck, you now have to pay federal

226

income tax on your earnings. And, if you live in one of the 46 states that require state income tax, you'll be paying that too.

By the way, you're responsible for paying federal income tax even if you're not living in the United States.

If you're a US citizen working abroad but earning a paycheck from a firm within the United States, you'll still have to pay federal income tax. Even if your paycheck is coming from a firm located in a foreign country, you'll still be paying federal income tax on your salary once it crosses a certain threshold.

At this point, the money that you've earned is now technically yours. As such, you can choose to either spend it or invest/ save it.

If you invest it, any returns you generate on your investment will be taxed at some point (via either taxes on capital gains if you happen to buy low and sell high, or taxes on income/ dividends if you choose to invest it in bonds/ income investments).

Even if you manage to hold on to your capital for the remainder of your life, when you pass and leave some money to your children/ loved ones, **it will be taxed again via estate taxes.**

By the way, this last step is technically a wealth tax since by this point your money is wealth, not income.

So, in this context, given the whole slew of taxes we've outlined, does a wealth tax of 10% on net wealth really seem so outlandish? Every $1 you own has already been taxed 7+ times.

Still not convinced?

Well, consider that the International Money Fund (the IMF) has been pushing for a wealth tax on net wealth since 2013. And lest you think the IMF is doing this out of an altruistic urge to give capital to the less fortunate, the IMF stated, point blank, that the goal was to use the capital as a means of shoring up sovereign finances (the Everything Bubble or sovereign debt bubble).

And, once again, the policy was sold as… being "for the public's good."

In this case, the public "good" meant the public's finances… as in the amount of debt politicians had generated by spending more money than their respective governments had collected via taxes (the taxes that those with some degree of wealth were already paying).

Oh, and by the way, this isn't about making the wealthy pay "their fair share," either. The IMF explicitly stated that the tax should apply to **all households with a positive net wealth.**

Put another way, provided the capital and assets you own add up to an amount greater than the debt you owe, the IMF thinks it'd be a good idea for you to hand over 10% of that amount.

And the IMF literally meant that it's a "good" idea in a moral sense. As soon as the IMF report titled *Taxing Times* was published, multiple establishment economists immediately hailed its proposal as "moral" and "right." In fact, the only real complaint from financial elites was that this scheme probably wouldn't work because people would try to get out of it.

Yes, establishment economists believe the problem with a 10% wealth tax is that people wouldn't want to pay it.

If you still think this is just theoretical moon-battery, consider that several developed countries have already adopted similar programs, taxing net wealth **annually**, albeit at a lower rate.

Again, these were not 3rd World dictatorships either, the countries in question were in Europe:

- Since 2011, France has imposed an annual tax between 0.5% and 1.5% of all wealth above €1.3 million. Those living in France are taxed on worldwide assets while those who live outside of France are taxed solely on assets located in France.

- Italy charges its citizens an annual tax of 0.76% on the purchase price of all real estate located outside the EU, as well as a tax of 0.15% on the fair value of all assets held abroad.

- Switzerland charges its citizens an annual wealth tax between 0.05% and 0.94% provided they have more than 100,000 Swiss Francs in net wealth.

My primary point is this: the fact the IMF is already promoting the notion of a one-off wealth tax as a means of accessing more capital to reduce sovereign debt loads indicates that this idea has been discussed at the highest levels in the US financial system.

All that the political class/ financial regulators need to pursue such a scheme is an excuse. When the Everything Bubble bursts and the financial system enters another crisis, they will have their excuse.

Politically, this policy will be sold as getting the wealthy to "pay their fair share," but in truth it's just another cash grab in a desperate attempt to reduce the leverage in the financial system.

At the end of the day, it all comes back to Chart 68. If that little dip in the dashed line represented the 2008 crisis… the crisis during which everyone thought the world was ending… you can only imagine what a significant bout of debt deflation would feel like.

Chart 68. Total US Debt Securities and Cash/ Cash Equivalents, Trillions US Dollars (1981-2016).

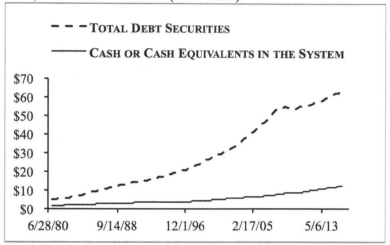

Note: Data adapted from Federal Reserve Bank of St. Louis (2017)[3,26]

Put simply, the problem with the US financial system today is that there's too little capital backstopping too much debt. So, when the Everything Bubble bursts, authorities will be doing everything they can to access more capital. This will eventually lead them to pursue Bail-Ins and Wealth Taxes.

The American public will undoubtedly push back against these policies. But in the end, they won't really have a choice.

After all, if your options are…

1) Agree to an extremely unpleasant option, which results in you losing *some* money.

2) Refuse to agree to option #1 and lose **everything**.

… which one will you end up choosing?

Good! God! Almighty!

REFERENCES

1. U.S. Bureau of Labor Statistics, Consumer Price Index for All Urban Consumers: Purchasing Power of the Consumer Dollar [CUUR0000SA0R], retrieved from FRED, Federal Reserve Bank of St. Louis; https://fred.stlouisfed.org/series/CUUR0000SA0R, September 2, 2017.

2. About Federal Reserve Bank Services. (2017). Retrieved from https://www.frbservices.org/aboutus/index.html

3. U.S. Bureau of Economic Analysis, Gross Domestic Product [GDP], retrieved from FRED, Federal Reserve Bank of St. Louis; https://fred.stlouisfed.org/series/GDP, September 4, 2017.

Board of Governors of the Federal Reserve System (US), All Sectors; Debt Securities and Loans; Liability, Level (DISCONTINUED) [TCMDO], retrieved from FRED, Federal Reserve Bank of St. Louis; https://fred.stlouisfed.org/series/TCMDO, September 4, 2017.

4. U.S. Bureau of Labor Statistics, Consumer Price Index for All Urban Consumers: All Items [CPIAUCSL], retrieved from FRED, Federal Reserve Bank of St. Louis; https://fred.stlouisfed.org/series/CPIAUCSL, September 4, 2017.

Board of Governors of the Federal Reserve System (US), 10-Year Treasury Constant Maturity Rate [DGS10], retrieved from FRED, Federal Reserve Bank of St. Louis; https://fred.stlouisfed.org/series/DGS10, September 4, 2017.

5. U.S. Department of the Treasury. Fiscal Service, Federal Debt: Total Public Debt [GFDEBTN], retrieved from FRED, Federal Reserve Bank of St. Louis; https://fred.stlouisfed.org/series/GFDEBTN,

September 3, 2017.

6. Federal Reserve Bank of St. Louis and U.S. Office of Management and Budget, Federal Debt: Total Public Debt as Percent of Gross Domestic Product [GFDEGDQ188S], retrieved from FRED, Federal Reserve Bank of St. Louis; https://fred.stlouisfed.org/series/GFDEGDQ188S, September 3, 2017.

7. Board of Governors of the Federal Reserve System (US), State and Local Governments, Excluding Employee Retirement Funds; Credit Market Instruments; Liability, Level [SLGSDODNS], retrieved from FRED, Federal Reserve Bank of St. Louis; https://fred.stlouisfed.org/series/SLGSDODNS, September 4, 2017.

Board of Governors of the Federal Reserve System (US), Nonfinancial corporate business; debt securities; liability, Level [NCBDBIA027N], retrieved from FRED, Federal Reserve Bank of St. Louis; https://fred.stlouisfed.org/series/NCBDBIA027N, September 4, 2017.

Board of Governors of the Federal Reserve System (US), Total Consumer Credit Owned and Securitized, Outstanding [TOTALSL], retrieved from FRED, Federal Reserve Bank of St. Louis; https://fred.stlouisfed.org/series/TOTALSL, September 4, 2017.

8. NASDAQ Financial Glossary. (2017). Retrieved from http://www.nasdaq.com/investing/glossary/e/economic-bubble

9. About the Fed. (2017). Retrieved from http://www.federalreserve.gov/aboutthefed/section2a.htm

10. NASDAQ OMX Group, NASDAQ Composite Index© [NASDAQCOM], retrieved from FRED, Federal Reserve Bank of St. Louis; with permission from

NASDAQ OMX Group, Inc. https://fred.stlouisfed.org/series/NASDAQCOM, September 4, 2017.

11. Board of Governors of the Federal Reserve System (US), Effective Federal Funds Rate [FEDFUNDS], retrieved from FRED, Federal Reserve Bank of St. Louis; https://fred.stlouisfed.org/series/FEDFUNDS, September 4, 2017.

12. U.S. Bureau of the Census, New One Family Houses Sold: United States [HSN1F], retrieved from FRED, Federal Reserve Bank of St. Louis; https://fred.stlouisfed.org/series/HSN1F, September 4, 2017

U.S. Bureau of the Census, Average Sales Price for New Houses Sold in the United States [ASPNHSUS], retrieved from FRED, Federal Reserve Bank of St. Louis; https://fred.stlouisfed.org/series/ASPNHSUS, September 4, 2017.

13. "Quarterly Report on Bank Derivatives Activities." *Office of the Comptroller of the Currency,* https://www.occ.gov/topics/capital-markets/financial-markets/derivatives/derivatives-quarterly-report.html

14. Board of Governors of the Federal Reserve System (US), 3-Month Treasury Bill: Secondary Market Rate [TB3MS], retrieved from FRED, Federal Reserve Bank of St. Louis; https://fred.stlouisfed.org/series/TB3MS, September 4, 2017.

15. U.S. Department of the Treasury, 2-Year High Quality Market (HQM) Corporate Bond Par Yield [HQMCB2YRP], retrieved from FRED, Federal Reserve Bank of St. Louis; https://fred.stlouisfed.org/series/HQMCB2YRP, September 4, 2017.

16. Board of Governors of the Federal Reserve System (US), 30-Year Treasury Constant Maturity Rate

[GS30], retrieved from FRED, Federal Reserve Bank of St. Louis; https://fred.stlouisfed.org/series/GS30, September 3, 2017.

17. U.S. Bureau of Economic Analysis, Corporate Profits After Tax (without IVA and CCAdj) [CP], retrieved from FRED, Federal Reserve Bank of St. Louis; https://fred.stlouisfed.org/series/CP, September 4, 2017.

Corporate Earnings Yield calculation based on stock prices as represented by the Wilshire 5000 (Full Cap) Total Market Index™, provided by Wilshire Associates®. [WILL5000PRFC], retrieved from FRED, Federal Reserve Bank of St. Louis; https://fred.stlouisfed.org/series/WILL5000PRFC, September 4, 2017.

18. Board of Governors of the Federal Reserve System (US), All Federal Reserve Banks: Total Assets [WALCL], retrieved from FRED, Federal Reserve Bank of St. Louis; https://fred.stlouisfed.org/series/WALCL, September 4, 2017.

"S&P 500 Historical Data." *Investing.com*, www.investing.com/indices/us-spx-500-historical-data

19. "Spain 10-Year Bond Yield." *Investing.com*, www.investing.com/rates-bonds/spain-10-year-bond-yield-historical-data

"Italy 10-Year Bond Yield." *Investing.com*, www.investing.com/rates-bonds/italy-10-year-bond-yield-historical-data

20. "Spain 3-Month Bond Yield." *Investing.com*, www.investing.com/rates-bonds/spain-3-month-bond-yield-historical-data

"Italy 3-Month Bond Yield." *Investing.com*, www.investing.com/rates-bonds/italy-3-month-bond-yield-historical-data

21. "Germany 3-Month Bond Yield." *Investing.com*, www.investing.com/rates-bonds/germany-3-month-bond-yield-historical-data

"Key ECB Interest Rates." *European Central Bank*, www.ecb.europa.eu/stats/policy_and_exchange_rates/key_ecb_interest_rates/html/index.en.html

22. OECD Economic Surveys, Japan, April 2017. www.oecd.org/eco/surveys/Japan-2017-OECD-economic-survey-overview.pdf Retrieved on September 4, 2017.

23. Board of Governors of the Federal Reserve System (US), Currency Component of M1 [CURRENCY], retrieved from FRED, Federal Reserve Bank of St. Louis; https://fred.stlouisfed.org/series/CURRENCY, September 4, 2017.

Board of Governors of the Federal Reserve System (US), Households and Nonprofit Organizations; Net Worth, Level [TNWBSHNO], retrieved from FRED, Federal Reserve Bank of St. Louis; https://fred.stlouisfed.org/series/TNWBSHNO, September 4, 2017.

Board of Governors of the Federal Reserve System (US), Nonfinancial Corporate Business; Net Worth, Level [TNWMVBSNNCB], retrieved from FRED, Federal Reserve Bank of St. Louis; https://fred.stlouisfed.org/series/TNWMVBSNNCB, September 4, 2017.

24. JP Morgan Chase & Co. (2016) *Form 10-K 2016*. Retrieved from SEC EDGAR website http://www.sec.gov/edgar.shtml

25. Mazzucco, Denise. "Historical CD Interest Rates – 1984-2016." *Bankrate,*

19 April 2016, http://www.bankrate.com/banking/cds/historical-cd-interest-rates-1984-2016/

26. Board of Governors of the Federal Reserve System (US), M2 Money Stock [M2SL], retrieved from FRED, Federal Reserve Bank of St. Louis; https://fred.stlouisfed.org/series/M2SL, September 4, 2017.

27. World Bank, Deposit Money Bank Assets to GDP for United Kingdom [DDDI02GBA156NWDB], retrieved from FRED, Federal Reserve Bank of St. Louis; https://fred.stlouisfed.org/series/DDDI02GBA156NWDB, September 4, 2017.

World Bank, Deposit Money Bank Assets to GDP for United States [DDDI02USA156NWDB], retrieved from FRED, Federal Reserve Bank of St. Louis; https://fred.stlouisfed.org/series/DDDI02USA156NWDB, September 4, 2017.

World Bank, Deposit Money Bank Assets to GDP for Greece [DDDI02GRA156NWDB], retrieved from FRED, Federal Reserve Bank of St. Louis; https://fred.stlouisfed.org/series/DDDI02GRA156NWDB, September 4, 2017.

World Bank, Deposit Money Bank Assets to GDP for Germany [DDDI02DEA156NWDB], retrieved from FRED, Federal Reserve Bank of St. Louis; https://fred.stlouisfed.org/series/DDDI02DEA156NWDB, September 4, 2017.

World Bank, Deposit Money Bank Assets to GDP for Spain [DDDI02ESA156NWDB], retrieved from FRED, Federal Reserve Bank of St. Louis; https://fred.stlouisfed.org/series/DDDI02ESA156NWDB,

September 4, 2017.

World Bank, Deposit Money Bank Assets to GDP for Japan [DDDI02JPA156NWDB], retrieved from FRED, Federal Reserve Bank of St. Louis; https://fred.stlouisfed.org/series/DDDI02JPA156NWDB, September 4, 2017.

World Bank, Deposit Money Bank Assets to GDP for Cyprus [DDDI02CYA156NWDB], retrieved from FRED, Federal Reserve Bank of St. Louis; https://fred.stlouisfed.org/series/DDDI02CYA156NWDB, September 4, 2017

ABOUT THE AUTHOR

Graham Summers, is a Fuqua Business School MBA graduate, with over 15 years of experience in business strategy, investment research, global consulting and business development.

Graham has been a C-level executive for over half his professional career. His experience within and beyond the financial field allows him to develop aggressive investment strategies that focus on market out-performance and high impact risk-adjusted returns. An acclaimed communicator and strategist, Graham's cutting edge business and research insights have been featured in several media outlets around the world including: CNN Money, Fox Business, Rolling Stone Magazine, Crain's New York Business, the New York Post, MoneyTalk Radio, and The Huffington Post among many others.

Graham is currently President and Chief Market Strategist of Phoenix Capital Research, a global investment research firm located in Washington, DC.